11/03

Body Marks

The Millbrook Press   Brookfield, Connecticut

Tattooing, Piercing, and Scarification

Kathlyn Gay and Christine Whittington

To my son, Douglas J. Gay, who prompted me to
think about proposing a book on body marks when
he told me about his classmate Christine Whittington
and her tattoos. — Kathlyn Gay

For Stephen Whittington, who is not inked but
appreciates my tattoos, and for Ed "Wiz" Dumont, who
gave me my first tattoo. — Christine Whittington

Cover photograph courtesy of The Image Bank

Photographs courtesy of Woodfin Camp & Associates: pp. 6 (© Catherine Karnow), 26 (© Loren McIntyre), 46
(© A. Ramey), 66 (© Betty Press), 67 (bottom © Betty Press), 70 (© James Wilson); Getty Images: pp. 8
(Hulton/Archive), 27 (Hulton/Archive), 55 (Hulton/Archive), 92 (© David McNew); AP/Wide World Photos: pp.
9, 12, 14–15, 18, 40, 44, 50, 59, 72, 75, 81, 82, 83, 84, 94; Corbis: pp. 11 (© Catherine Karnow), 48 (© AFP),
69 (© Philip Gould); Magnum Photos: pp. 13 (© Steve McCurry), 23 (© Steve McCurry), 52 (© Alex Webb);
Liaison: p. 16 (© Bill Swersey); Institut für Ur-und Frühgeschichte (© Dr. Konrad Spindler): p. 20; Christine
Whittington: p. 28; Tattoo Archive, Berkeley, CA: pp. 32, 34; Art Resource, NY: pp. 36 (Smithsonian American Art
Museum, Washington, D.C.), 62 (Werner Forman); PhotoEdit: p. 38 (© David Young-Wolff); © 2000 Patricia
Steur: p. 42; National Geographic Society Image Collection: p. 67 (top © Jodi Cobb); © Joe
Satterwhite/Michigan Tattoo Company: p. 80 (all)
Illustrations pp. 57–58 by Sharon Lane Holm.

Library of Congress Cataloging-in-Publication Data
Gay, Kathlyn.
Body marks : tattooing, piercing, and scarification / by Kathlyn Gay and Christine Whittington.
p. cm.
Includes bibliographical references and index.
Summary: Discusses the history of various forms of body marking, current popularity of body piercing and tat-
toos, how and why these are done, and some things to think about before choosing to be pierced or tattooed.
ISBN 0-7613-2352-X (lib. bdg.) 0-7613-1742-2 (pbk.)
1. Body marking—Juvenile literature. 2. Body piercing—Juvenile literature. 3. Tattooing—Juvenile
literature. 4. Scarification (Body marking)—Juvenile literature. [1. Body marking. 2. Body piercing. 3. Tattooing.]
I. Whittington, Christine. II. Title.
GN419.5 .G39 2002   391.6'5—dc21   2001043462

Published by The Millbrook Press, Inc.
2 Old New Milford Road
Brookfield, Connecticut 06804
www.millbrookpress.com

Contents

Body Decorations

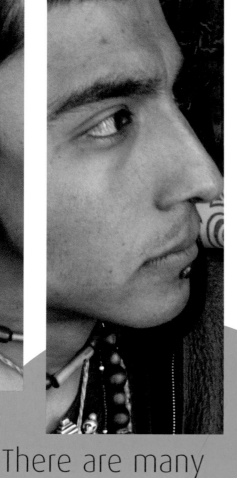

There are many different ways that men and women from all over the world decorate their skin today—from tattoos and body piercings to brandings and scars.

and Modifications

One of the most famous body marks displayed worldwide is the anchor tattoo on the oversized forearm of the cartoon character Popeye the Sailorman. His image was first created in 1929 by cartoonist Elzie Segar, who died in 1938. Popeye's character has been kept alive by other illustrators and can be seen in comic books sold around the world, in cartoons, on postage stamps and posters, on clothing, and through animated toys and countless other items. He's depicted in a feature film (played by actor Robin Williams), and immortalized with statues and, yes, tattoos.

Popeye's tattoo image, as well as other tattoos, represents just one type of body art. From business executives to dishwashers, from librarians to football players, from teenagers to octogenarians, people express themselves not only with tattoos but also with body piercings and with brandings created by searing the skin with hot metal so that it will form a scar.

Scars are also created by cutting the skin and letting it heal. But scarification, as it's called, is considered a more radical form of body decoration than tattooing or piercing. So is the practice of implanting, which involves making a shallow cut in the skin, inserting an object, and sewing the skin over it. The body can also be modified by plastic surgery, excessive bodybuilding exercises, and constant dieting—practices that are widespread today. Restrictive clothing (like corsets and head bindings) was common in the past and is sometimes used in modern times to modify the body. But this book focuses primarily on "skin art"—marking the skin with tattoos, piercings, scarification, and branding.

Ebb and Flow of Body Art

Millions of people worldwide adorn themselves with a great variety of body decorations, particularly tattoos and piercings. But in the Western world the practice of tattooing the body has gained and faded in popularity over the centuries. For example, during the late 1800s, tattooing became popular among members of "high society," including women and royalty, in England and the United States.

About the same time, the invention of the tattoo machine allowed tattooing to be done more quickly and cheaply. Tattooing became affordable and popular among working-class people. Newspaper and magazine articles began to link tattooing with criminals and loose morals, and the popularity of tattooing among the upper classes declined. Tattooists continued to practice, but they set up their businesses in the back rooms of stores or shops, usually located in what were considered undesirable parts of town, like New York's Bowery, Chicago's skid row, Boston's Scollay Square, or other entertainment districts of port cities where sailors gathered.

A tattoo art studio in the Bowery district of New York City around 1935

During the 1960s and 1970s, rock-and-roll musicians, bikers, and others who wanted to defy accepted dress and cultural patterns began to prominently display their tattoos—or in their jargon, their "tats" or "ink." Today, people with tattoos, body piercings, and brands are everywhere. They are shown in advertisements, on television shows, and in magazine and newspaper photographs. Even a glamorous toy icon, Barbie, comes with temporary tattoos.

Celebrity Body Art....................

Helping to increase the popularity of body art are hundreds of celebrities—athletes, musicians, sports stars, models, actors and actresses, and politicians. Examples include:

- Boxing legend Muhammad Ali's daughter, Laila, who made her own debut as a boxer in 1999, has a braceletlike tattoo on her wrist.
- Four-time Olympic gold medal swimmer Amy Van Dyken displays a tattoo of the Olympic Games logo on her calf.
- Actress Drew Barrymore is tattooed with a blue moon, a butterfly, angels, and flowers.
- Singer Britney Spears wears a silver and turquoise navel ring, and has a fairy with black wings tattooed at the base of her spine.
- British actor Jude Law has words from the Beatles' song "Sexie Sadie" tattooed on his arm.
- Actress Julia Roberts has Chinese characters tattooed on her shoulder.
- Actor Ben Affleck is tattooed with a variety of designs on his back and shoulders.

The actress Angelina Jolie, who has numerous tattoos, wears a tribal dragon, drawing attention to this popular style of body art.

- Actor and musician Mark Wahlberg wears a rosary tattoo around his neck and tattoos on both shoulders and ankles.
- Talk show hostess Rosie O'Donnell has an ankle tattoo of a cross and flowers.
- Actor Johnny Depp got a "Winona Forever" tattoo referring to actress Winona Rider.
- Boxer Mike Tyson celebrates his heroes with tattoos: Mao Zedong's face on his upper right arm, tennis champion Arthur Ashe's face on the left arm, and Che Guevara's face on his stomach.
- Singer Janet Jackson reportedly has genital, nipple, and tongue piercings along with various tattoos.

The list goes on, and most of the named celebrities plus many more can be viewed showing off their body art on various Web sites, in videos, and in publicity photos for advertisements, fan magazines, and other publications.

When sports stars, television or movie stars, and popular musicians appear with body adornments, they convey messages that may be interpreted in different ways, raising questions such as:

- Are body markings acceptable?
- Is body art the thing to do?
- Are tattoos and piercings the latest style in body wear?
- Do tattoos and piercings indicate a person is "tough" and rebellious?
- Where do people get their body marks?
- Why are tattoos and piercings popular today?

Popularity of Body Art

As body marks and modifications have gained acceptance in the United States, what has become the most common forms of adornment? Piercings for belly button jewelry certainly make the list. The owner of a body art studio in central Florida, for example, says that each week he sees dozens of teenagers who come in to inquire about or to get navel piercings.

The multipierced look also has become common among teenagers and young adults, who wear not only navel jewelry and multiple earrings but also

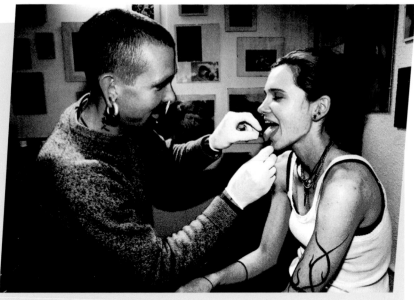

At a body-piercing studio in San Francisco, a customer gets her tongue pierced, which is a big trend among young adults in many countries.

eyebrow rings and tongue studs. However, employees who wear multiple piercings may be required to remove them if they want to keep their jobs.

When it comes to tattoos, some of the most popular designs are on studio walls and in artists' portfolios. These illustrations, called "flash," are sets of pictures drawn by specific artists and reproduced and distributed so that they can be used to tattoo customers at many shops.

Tribal markings, such as the predominantly black, one-dimensional tattoos of traditional cultures in the Pacific Islands or among Native Americans, are popular, as are dragons. The traditional roses, hearts, eagles, and people's names are also common.

According to an artist in Radford, Virginia, who tattoos many Radford University students, "The more popular tattoos are butterflies for the ladies and the Chinese and Japanese characters, or Kanji, for the guys." A reporter for the university newspaper noted, "The butterfly is usually placed on the lower back or leg while the Kanji on the upper arm or chest. The Kanji can have various meanings from regret to vitality."[1]

Women in Cincinnati, Ohio, tend to choose flower tattoos,"and they generally want them on their lower leg or ankle," according to a news report. "For men, the more popular tattoos include tribal bands or animals on their upper or lower arms."[2]

Across the United States there are variations on what is popular in a particular community or region of the country. It could be sunbursts, angels, barbed wire, happy faces, zodiac signs, and even eyeliner tattoos.

Why Body Markings and Modifications?

Although many people get a tattoo, piercing, or brand simply to be in style or to be trendy, individuals mark or modify their bodies for a great variety of reasons. Some people are motivated by the desire to be in control. They believe they should be able to decorate their bodies any way they please and should not have to explain or justify their choices. Others contend that their tattoos and piercings represent who they are and emphasize their individuality and creativity. Still others, sometimes called "modern primitives," want to establish a link with ancient people or traditional cultures as a response to what they perceive as the superficiality of Western society.

In Las Vegas, a popular city to get a tattoo, the owner of a tattoo studio made this observation about those who seek his services: "A lot of kids are getting tattoos; it's like a coming of age kind of thing. A lot of parents are bringing kids in, too." He noted that those aged twenty-five and older "usually have specific reasons" for getting their tattoos. "If you could just tape the conversations here on a Saturday night, it's a lot like being in a doctor's office. The stories range from sad to funny."[3]

Vince Cancasci in Ventura, California, was like many other teenagers

Fred Durst of the rock band Limp Bizkit shows off his tattoos at the MTV Video Music Awards in 2000. Rock stars have greatly increased the popularity of tattooing and piercing in recent years.

when he got his first tattoo. At age sixteen he wanted "to impress others— seem like a tough guy." He said he had "seen older people with tattoos and thought that they were so intimidating because they had ink." But he admits, "I was scared out of my mind. I got myself all worked up to the point where I passed out in the chair . . . it was embarrassing to say the least!"

Vince, now in his twenties, has fifteen tattoos, and he says all of them "except for the very first one mean something deep to me. They all represent a part of my life that I always want to remember. Some people write in a diary. I write on myself. There are four on my body that I placed there to let certain people know how much they mean to me. My wife, my sister, and my kids."[4]

Some people insist that being tattooed is spiritual, a way to get in touch with oneself. Maureen Mercury, author of *Pagan Fleshworks,* contends that tattoos, body piercings, brands, and implants help people connect with and hear the voices of their souls or psyches. In her view, "We are modern people . . . desperate to find our own inner images of resonance that tell us who we are. We are searching, through our bodies, for the sounds and images of our own personal gods that have all but gone silent."[5] With photographs by the well- known body modification artist Steve Haworth, Mercury's book shows and describes how people create their own rituals and express their inner voices and the "divine within."

Among a relatively small group of evangelical Christians, tattooing is a way to seek converts. These evangelists display their tattoos, which include pictures of Jesus, scenes of the Last Supper, crosses, and other Christian symbols. According to a *Christianity Today* article, one young man, Derrick Rachul, went to Hawaii with a group intent on evangelizing surfers. Rachul said he "met a guy that had a whole pile of tattoos—demons, naked women, the whole bit . . . He noticed my tattoo and asked me about it. I told him I'm a Christian and talked about what it represents."[6]

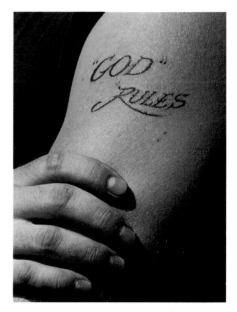

The increasing popularity of the Christian punk rock and hard-core music scene is also being reflected in the rise of religious tattoos.

Whatever the reasons for tattooing, piercing, or other body modifications, the fact remains that for millennia people around the world have decorated their bodies. According to an introductory statement for a body art exhibit, shown from November 1999 through May 2000 at New York's American Museum of Natural History, "there is no known culture in which people do not paint, pierce, tattoo, reshape, or simply adorn their bodies. Whether with permanent marks like tattoos

TATTOOS

Tattoo lovers gather at the First Annual New York City Tattoo Convention at Roseland Ballroom in 1998.

or scars, or temporary decorations like makeup, clothing, and hairstyles, body art is a way of signaling an individual's place in society, marking a special moment, celebrating a transition in life, or simply following a fashion."[7]

Today, body decorations are frequently inspired by creative practices of the past. Some of those practices stem from ancient times, dating from even before recorded history.

From the Stone Age

Animal-style tattoo art is visible
on this three-thousand-year-old mummy
found in Siberia. The Pazyryks might have
believed that when tattooed with a picture
of an animal, a person gained
that animal's power.

to the Voyages
of Exploration

t is virtually certain that human skin, bones, teeth, and hair were the first . . . canvases for artistic expression," writes archaeologist and prehistoric art scholar Paul G. Bahn.[1] For thousands of years, people around the world have painted their faces and bodies to enhance their eyes, eyebrows, lips, or other features.

Prehistoric people may have first begun to mark the human body for practical purposes. Red and yellow ochre and other mineral pigments that were found in human burial sites dating from tens of thousands of years ago may have been used to preserve the human body and neutralize odors, in the same way they were used to preserve animal skins.

People may have used the pigments on the sick or dying, as well as the dead, for their medicinal properties, thus associating body painting with rituals related to death. According to Bahn, "If members of Australia's Arunta tribe felt ill, their bodies were rubbed with red ochre, while the Sioux Dakota used to paint women and children red before they died."[2]

Bahn also believes that prehistoric people colored their bodies for pure aesthetic pleasure, noting that many of the world's peoples today use paint to "accentuate their natural traits." For example, "the Colorado Indians of Ecuador paint designs on their face and arms for beautification, while the Nuba of the Sudan do the same to celebrate, emphasize, and enhance a healthy and strong body."[3] Unlike animals, whose use of body adornment is instinctive (the male peacock spreading his tail, for example), humans adorn their bodies deliberately.

Applying facial and body painting has long accompanied rituals. An ancient method of body painting is *mehndi*, or the art of applying henna, a practice that continues around the world today. The earliest reference to the use of henna is on a Syrian tablet dating from 2100 B.C. The tablet was inscribed with a legend that tells about a goddess of fertility and battle whose hands were decorated with henna. The legend also describes the use of henna for bridal adornment.[4]

Henna is a small shrub, *Lawsonia inermis*, that grows in India, Pakistan, Iran, and North Africa. The leaves of the henna plant or shrub are dried, ground into a powder, then mixed with water, lemon or lime juice, or oil to form a dye paste. Tea or other natural ingredients may be added also to darken the dye.

A woman in Massachusetts creates beautiful and intricate designs on a customer's hands using the ancient art of mehndi.

Mehndi artists often experiment with ingredients for the henna paste and apply it with tools, such as tooth-picks, orange sticks, cake decorators, or funnels made from plastic bags. The mehndi artist draws intricate designs with the paste, which is left on for several hours, then peeled or scraped off to reveal a reddish or brownish-orange design.[5]

Other types of body painting also have ancient origins. Consider the Olmec, an indigenous group (those native to the land) who lived on the coastal plains of Mexico and worshiped the jaguar. Their descendants today prepare for a rain dance by painting their bodies with clay and stamping jaguar spots onto their skin with bottle tops dipped in ashes.

In Papua New Guinea, indigenous people paint themselves black and white to resemble skeletons, for an effect that Dutch author and social anthropologist Rufus Camphausen says "attests to the ability of many tribal people to see beyond, or into, normal physical appearances."[6]

The ritual of painting the skin has carried over to the present day and is popular at numerous functions in the United States. Face painting at festivals, fairs, and school activities is a common occurrence. Sports fans also follow the custom of painting the skin to show team loyalty. Some male baseball fans, for example, strip to the waist and paint their faces and chests with team colors or symbols.

Ancient Tattooing

Archaeologists believe that puncturing the skin with a sharp object in order to introduce color— in other words, tattooing—may have been another very early human practice. Researchers at archaeological sites in Europe and elsewhere have found possible tattooing tools, such as disks made of clay and red ochre pierced with holes, along with bone needles that fit into the holes. Prehistoric people may have used the needles to pick up pigment from the red ochre in the disk and transfer the color to the skin.[7]

Investigators searching caves in France, Portugal, Romania, and Scandinavia have discovered bowls containing traces of color, needles, and small figures with marks that may represent tattooing. A discovery in French caves revealed hollow engraved bone tubes with traces of powdered pigment. Human figurines buried along with bodies in graves bear traces of painting or geometric marks that suggest piercing and coloring of the skin.[8] Did the body, as well as cave walls, serve as a canvas?

The Iceman

Researchers can be certain that tattooing existed in a past culture only when they are able to examine tattooed individuals preserved as mummies. Tattooed mummies have been found throughout the world, including western Europe, Egypt, central Asia, Greenland, and Chile.

In 1991 hikers in the Ötztaler Alps between Austria and Italy discovered the top half of a mummified body sticking out of a glacier. Preserved by the

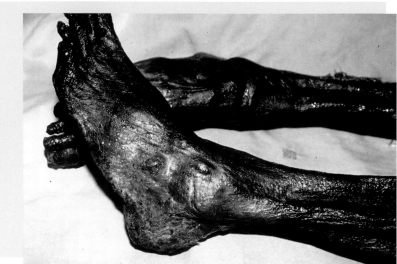

Here, you can see a grouping of three linear tattoos on the outside of Ötzi's left ankle.

ice and snow, the body was that of a Neolithic hunter, the oldest mummified body found thus far and estimated to have lived 5,300 years ago. Nicknamed Ötzi or the Iceman, the mummy was taken to a laboratory in the South Tyrolean Museum of Archaeology in Bolzano, Italy. Forensic scientists began to piece together his life, his final hours, and the meaning of the tattoos on his body.

In August 2001, X rays uncovered the cause of Ötzi's death—a flint arrowhead buried within his left shoulder. Ötzi had been shot from behind, and died from blood loss after escaping from his attacker.[9]

Among Ötzi's most intriguing features are more than fifty tattoos arranged in fifteen groups of lines on his back and legs.[10] Most of the tattoo groups consist of parallel lines, but two, on the knee and lower leg, are crosses. Archaeologist Konrad Spindler believes that the distinctive blue tint of Ötzi's tattoos indicate that charcoal was probably used to make them.[11]

Ötzi may have been tattooed for medical rather than decorative reasons because of the basic shape of his tattoos. Also, the tattoos were on parts of his body that are ordinarily hidden by clothing. One scientist noticed that the placement of Ötzi's tattooed lines were similar to traditional acupuncture points—places on the body where fine needles are inserted into the skin to stimulate channels of energy and to heal various conditions. Experts from acupuncture societies confirmed that nine of the tattoo groups were near acupuncture points, and that three others may also have been related to acupuncture.[12]

Why would Ötzi need acupuncture therapy? X rays indicate that eight of his tattoo groups are located near areas where he suffered from arthritis: his lower spine and his hip, knee, and ankle joints.[13] One of Ötzi's cross-shaped tattoos shows a "perfect hit on the 'Liver 8' acupuncture point, used to treat abdominal disorders."[14] No doubt Ötzi felt the need for some relief in this area, as he had whipworm eggs in his colon, and had been using charcoal and a birch fungus remedy from his "traveling medicine kit" as natural antibiotics and laxatives.[15]

Tattooing in Egypt

Tattooed mummies have also been exhumed in Egypt. Egyptian tattoos were made with blackish-blue pigment applied with a pricking device such as fish bones set into a handle.

So far, all the Egyptian mummies with tattoos that have been found are female. Amunet, a priestess of the goddess Hathor at Thebes during the Eleventh Dynasty (2160–1994 B.C.), is the best preserved; she was excavated in A.D. 1923 along with two other tattooed mummies.[16]

Randomly placed dots and dashes adorn Amunet's body, and an elliptical pattern appears on her lower abdomen beneath her navel. The second mummy, probably a dancer, has diamond-shaped patterns of dots on her arms and chest plus a curved scar across her lower abdomen. Similar tattoos decorate the third mummy.[17]

The Egyptians did not have a word for tattooing, nor did they leave any written records about it. Tattooing may have come to Egypt from the African kingdom of Nubia. Excavations at a Nubian village have revealed a female mummy from 2000 B.C. The Nubian mummy's tattoos are similar to Amunet's, consisting of abstract patterns of dots and dashes.[18]

The Pazyryks

In 1948, Soviet archaeologist Sergei Ivanovich Rudenko uncovered the tomb of a tattooed Pazyryk mummy, an Iron Age horseman who lived 2,400 years ago. The body was preserved by the permafrost in the high Altai Mountains of the western and southern Siberian steppes, just north of the border between China and Russia. The mummified Pazyryk chieftain was a powerfully built man who was about fifty years old when he died. He was tattooed with a variety of fantastic creatures, including a donkey, a ram, two deer, griffins, monsters, and a fish, in twisted positions characteristic of Scythian "animal style" art.

Archaeologists believe that the chieftain acquired the tattoos when he was a younger—and thinner—man, because the designs stretched as the chieftain increased in size. In addition to these elaborate tattoos, the chieftain also had a series of simple circles tattooed along his spine. Like Ötzi's tattoos, these may have been pain relievers for his back, a remedy that Siberian tribes practice today.[19]

In the summer of 1993, archaeologists discovered another Pazyryk mummy in the Siberian Umok plateau, this time that of a young woman. Her attire and elaborately decorated casket clearly indicated her high status, as did the young woman's tattooed arms, adorned with creatures similar to those on the body of the chieftain.[20]

Other Body Modifications

Prehistoric people practiced other forms of body modification, such as filing and decorating teeth; sometimes, teeth were even removed. People decorated their teeth four thousand years ago in Japan and in Mesolithic India. The Maya, who lived in the area that now includes Mexico, Guatemala, Belize, and Honduras, commonly drilled holes in the visible surfaces of their teeth to accommodate inlays of gold or semiprecious gems such as jadeite or turquoise.[21]

Changing the shape of the head was also a common practice in many cultures. This involved binding or applying pressure to the heads of infants before their skulls had fully formed. Archaeologists have recovered elongated skulls from the Ica area of Peru, and there is some evidence that this practice existed even among the Neanderthals.[22] An exhibit at the University of Iowa Medical Museum notes that "aristocratic ancient Greek and Roman families" practiced skull modification as did "North, Central, and South American Indians," as well as Africans and Europeans. "In areas of Holland, for example, tight-fitting caps worn by women throughout their lives created a unique head shape."[23]

Foot binding, a Chinese practice that began in the tenth century and lasted until the early 1900s, was used to modify the shape and size of girls' feet.

The Chinese considered tiny feet desirable in women. According to a study led by Professor Steven R. Cummings, M.D., of the University of California at San Francisco, "girls' feet were bound so tightly and early in life that they were unable to dance and had difficulty walking. By the time a girl turned three years old, all her toes but the first were broken, and her feet were bound tightly with cloth strips to keep her feet from growing larger than about 4 inches (10 cm). The practice would cause the soles of feet to bend in extreme concavity."[24]

Another body modifying practice, often referred to as neck elongation, has a long history and is still prevalent among women of the Padaung of Myanmar (formerly Burma), many of whom now live in Thailand. In early childhood, girls begin to wear brass rings around their necks, and these are periodically increased "to a maximum of thirty, until a woman marries," notes Discovery's "Human Canvas" Web site exhibit. "European explorers who first encountered the Padaung believed that the rings actually stretched their necks, but X rays of Padaung women have shown that this is actually an illusion. Instead, the rings, which can weigh more than 20 pounds (9 kg), gradually force down the clavicles and ribcage, until they are reshaped in an unnatural, inverted V-shape."[25]

These women are wearing brass rings that ultimately force down their rib cage and create the illusion of an elongated neck. The number of rings that each woman wears reflects her status and the amount of respect bestowed upon her family.

Ancient Greek and Roman Body Marks

In ancient Greece and Rome, tattoos were seldom ornamental. Rather, they were marks of ownership for slaves and punishment for criminals and, therefore, a disgrace. The Greeks may have learned tattooing practices from their neighbors to the north, especially the Thracians, who lived in the area that is

now Bulgaria and western Turkey. Herodotus, a Greek historian of the fifth century B.C., wrote that the Persian king Xerxes tattooed his slaves and Greek prisoners of war. Greeks used tattooing from the fifth century on, apparently adopting the Persian tattooing practice, which signified punishment, degradation, and permanent ownership.[26]

The first reference to tattooing in Greek literature is as *stigmatias*, or "a marked slave." (In English, the word *stigma* comes from the Greek and indicates shame or discredit.) Greek slaves were marked with descriptions of their crimes tattooed on their foreheads, including in one case the words, "Stop me, I'm a runaway."[27]

Romans learned about tattooing from the Greeks, and continued the practice of marking slaves. Romans also continued to use the word *stigmata* to denote tattooing. The oldest known description of stigmata is in a medical text, *Medicae artis principes*, by the sixth-century Roman physician Aetius. He describes stigmata as "things inscribed on the face or some other part of the body, for example on the hands of soldiers." Aetius also describes the operation: "Apply by pricking the places with needles, wiping away the blood, and rubbing in first the juice of leek, then [the ink] preparation."[28] According to tattoo artist and historian Steve Gilbert, Aetius's recipe for ink included pinewood, corroded bronze, gall (from a gallnut or insect infestation on a tree), and vitriol (oil).[29]

The military writer Vegetius described how soldiers were inscribed with "permanent dots in the skin," indicating the name or numbers of their units so that they could be identified if they tried to desert.[30] In the movie *Gladiator*, released in 2000, the gladiator Maximus scrapes tattooed initials SPQR from his arm. SPQR stands for "Senate and People of Rome" (*Senatus populusque Romanus*), and is intended to identify Maximus as an army deserter because SPQR was the "mark of the legion" tattooed or branded on Roman soldiers. However, the practice described by Vegetius occurred later than the film's A.D. 180 setting.[31] In addition, even though most gladiators in Roman times were slaves, archaeologists do not believe that a slave would be tattooed with the letters SPQR.[32]

Religious Tattooing

Toward the end of the Roman Empire, Constantine, who became the first Christian emperor in 324 B.C., decreed that criminals should not be tattooed on the face but on the hands or calves in order to preserve the image of the divine, as represented by the face. Christians also had themselves tattooed with religious emblems or the name of Jesus.

Essentially, religious tattooing died out in most of Europe between the twelfth and sixteenth centuries A.D., but medieval Christian crusaders kept the tattooing tradition alive. When they reached the Holy Land, they had symbols tattooed on their bodies as souvenirs of their crusades. Years later, William Lithgow, who made a pilgrimage to the Holy Land in 1612, describes being tattooed by a Christian at Bethlehem with the name of Jesus, a cross, and the crown of King James. Similar accounts of tattooing in Palestine are recorded in the journals of other Christian pilgrims and crusaders, and the practice has continued into the twenty-first century.[33]

When historian John Carswell visited Jerusalem in 1956, he found a tattoo artist, Jacob Razzouk, who was using his family's seventeenth-century woodblocks with carved tattoo designs, serving as both a design catalogue and a guide for the tattoo needle. Razzouk told Carswell that tattooing is a seasonal trade, with the peak period at Easter, "when whole families are tattooed simultaneously." Carswell reports that "all Coptic [Egyptian Christian] pilgrims are virtually obliged to be tattooed as their compatriots would not consider a pilgrimage valid without this visible sign." Razzouk's customers included pilgrims of many denominations, as confirmed by Armenian, Syrian, Latin, Abyssinian, and Slav—and one Hebrew—designs in the collection.[34]

Body Marks in the Western World

European explorers and missionaries in the Americas reported widespread tattooing, piercing, and branding among Native Americans. Most societies in ancient Mesoamerica (an area that encompasses most of Mexico and part of Central America) practiced piercing or perforation to induce bloodletting, decorative piercing, scarification, and probably tattooing. As with other cultures, these practices were often important for religious and ritual purposes. Nobles pierced or perforated their flesh to sacrifice their blood to the gods.

The Maya practiced what seems to be a record number of body modifications. These included tattooing; piercing and decorating the lips, noses, ears, and genitals; head deformation; enlargement of the bridge of the nose; creation of crossed eyes in children by hanging a ball of wax between the eyes; scalding and plucking male facial hair; filing teeth and inlaying them with precious stones; and body painting for status, pleasure, and insect repellent.

Friar Diego de Landa, a Spanish Franciscan priest who became bishop of Yucatán, traveled through Central America between 1549 and 1562. He reported that the Maya cut pictures in the skin and darkened them with ink. Mayans who did not submit to tattooing were ridiculed, but tattooing on the face was a disgrace and was used to punish thieves.

Different cultures display many different types of body decorations. This man from the Amazon in Brazil displays very colorful and dramatic adornments, such as piercings on his face and ritualistic markings along his body.

Landa also noted that the Maya sacrificed their own blood by cutting their ears or perforating their cheeks and tongues.[35] The Maya even had a Perforator God, who symbolized the lancet used for piercing.[36] Sculptures from the western Mexican Nayarit culture show people piercing their cheeks with large sticks and pointed bones as a mourning ritual.

Tattooing among North American Indians was common and often served as an indication of bravery. Among the Osage, a skull tattooed on a warrior's back or chest indicated he had been successful in battle. When Omaha men committed brave deeds, their daughters received the honors with tattoos on their backs or breasts. The Inuit tattooed marks on their bodies to keep track of the number of whales they killed, and Inuit women's chins were tattooed to indicate marital status and group identity. Among the Ontario Iroquois, tattooing indicated high status.[37]

This is a studio portrait from around 1860 of a woman who was captured by Native Americans and then sold to the Mojave tribe. They reportedly treated her kindly, but tattooed her chin with the mark of a slave.

Seventeenth-century French explorers reported that Huron warriors "paint themselves various colors, a fashion which seems horrible to us, but beautiful to them," including nose and eyes painted blue, eyebrows and cheeks painted black, and red and blue stripes from ear to mouth or ear to ear across the forehead.[38]

Although the desire to decorate oneself is universal, the types of body art people use depend upon their culture and place in history. Thus what may seem like "normal" body marking practices among members of one group will frequently be rejected or banned completely by another group. Nevertheless, as Paul Bahn writes, "one need only reflect on how much prominence, even in modern, supposedly sophisticated societies, is still given to make-up, hairstyles, body-piercing and tattoos to realize that the deep-seated urge to decorate the human skin has never left us."[39] Indeed, it may be this innate urge to decorate our bodies that has enabled tattooing, piercing, and other forms of body marks to enter modern culture.

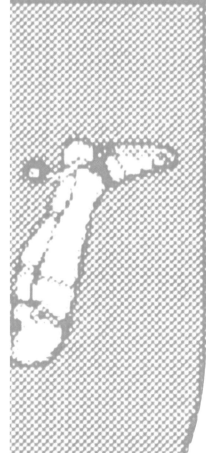

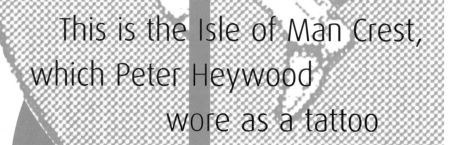

This is the Isle of Man Crest, which Peter Heywood wore as a tattoo

the Mainstream

n 1792, nineteen-year-old British Navy midshipman Peter Heywood was a prisoner aboard H.M.S. *Hector*, anchored in Portsmouth, England. He was awaiting trial for his part in the infamous mutiny against Captain William Bligh aboard H.M.S. *Bounty*. Heywood, from a prominent family, had joined the *Bounty*'s breadfruit-gathering expedition to Tahiti when he was fourteen years old, and he hardly expected to find himself in trouble five years later.

Like most of his fellow crewmen, Heywood had acquired tattoos. In a letter to his mother, he explained that he wanted to gain the "friendship and esteem" of the Tahitians:

> [the] more a man or woman there is tattooed, the more respect is paid them; and a person who has none of these marks is looked upon as bearing a most indignant badge of disgrace, and considered as a mere outcast of society. You may suppose, then, that my disposition would not suffer me to be long out of fashion. I always made it a maxim when I was in Rome to act as Rome did, provided it did not interfere with my morals or religion.[1]

Although Heywood was convicted of mutiny, he was not hanged. He was pardoned on October 24, 1792, and went on to have a distinguished naval career.

Even before Heywood's experiences with tattooing, British Captain (then Lieutenant) James Cook and his crew had encountered the practice of tattooing during their voyage to the Pacific between 1768 and 1771. The British Admiralty had selected Lieutenant Cook to lead an expedition to observe the transit of Venus across the Sun. According to the Web site of Great Britain's National Maritime Museum, Cook was also "given a secret mission to find the Southern Continent," which many people believed existed.[2] Joseph Banks, a naturalist, accompanied Cook to record descriptions of all plants, animals, minerals, and other natural resources they encountered.

In 1769, Cook's ship, *Endeavour*, reached the island of Tahiti. Banks not only recorded information about plants and animals but also made many observations about the lives and customs of the Tahitians, including tattooing. He described the methods and appearance of the Tahitians' "tattows":

> This they do by inlaying the color black under their skins in such a manner as to be indelible; everyone is marked thus in different parts of his body according maybe to his humor or different circumstances of his life . . . . All the islanders I have seen agree in having their buttocks covered with a deep black; over this most have arches drawn one over another as high as their short ribs . . . .[3]

Banks noted that tattooing was done between the ages of fourteen and sixteen, and described the tattooing of the buttocks of a fourteen-year-old girl: "For some time she bore it with great resolution, but afterwards began to complain and in a little time grew so outrageous that all the threats and force her friends could use could hardly oblige her to endure it."[4] In other words, although the tattooing was a painful ordeal for the girl, because of the Tahitians' tradition, she was expected to suffer through it.

When *Endeavour* left Tahiti, it sailed south, arriving in New Zealand, homeland of the Maori, in early October 1769. When a hostile group of Maori attacked, the British shot and killed a tribesman; Banks observed that the dead man "was tattooed on the face and on one cheek only in spiral lines very regularly formed,"[5] which is a description of moko, Maori facial tattooing that is still done today. Banks's scientific illustrator, Sydney Parkinson, made drawings of the Maoris' moko tattoos and of their tattooing instruments, which survive in his *Journal of a Voyage to the South Seas*, published in 1773.[6] Banks returned to England where, according to tattoo artist and historian Steve Gilbert, he "was much in demand as a guest at fashionable dinner parties, where he thrilled British socialites with tales of stormy seas, exotic islands, and tattooed cannibals."[7]

With their exotic tales and illustrations, the *Endeavour* crew introduced the onomatopoeic word "tattoo" or "tattow," as Banks spelled it, to the British. (Tattoo comes from the Polynesian *tatu* or *tatau*, meaning "to mark" or "to strike.") Cook also brought to England a tattooed Tahitian, Omai, who became a "national treasure, . . . a hero, . . . and a box-office hit." [8] More fortunate than other tattooed visitors to England, Omai returned home on Captain Cook's third voyage.

Cook's tattooed crew so intrigued British sailors, including those who would later sail on H.M.S. *Bounty*, that within a few years tattooing became a British Navy tradition. Almost all of the twenty-five *Bounty* mutineers were tattooed.[9] As souvenirs of their travels, many British sailors acquired tattoos on board ship or in foreign seaports. Tattooing also became popular among the British royalty and upper classes. In 1862 the Prince of Wales visited the Holy Land and had the Jerusalem Cross tattooed on his arm, and later when he became King Edward VII, he acquired additional tattoos.[10] Aristocratic women were also tattooed, although not as extensively as men. Lady Randolph Churchill, for example, was adorned with a serpent around her wrist, which she later covered up with a heavy bracelet when tattooing became a practice of commoners.

Tattooing in the United States

By the end of the 1800s, London tattoo artist George Burchett had become known as the "King of Tattooists," serving clients such as King Alfonso of Spain and King Frederick IX of Denmark.[11] As tattooing gained popularity in England, its appeal "jumped the pond" to the United States. Descriptions of tattooing appear in journals, diaries, and letters of American sailors and their wives written during the late-eighteenth and early-nineteenth centuries. They are also mentioned in Seaman's Protection Act certificates, which were issued beginning in 1796. These certificates identified American sailors in order to protect them from impressment (forced service) on British ships. They list each sailor's name, date and place of birth, height, complexion, and distinguishing marks, such as scars, deformities, and tattoos.[12]

Tattooing moved beyond the seas and ships, when professional tattoo artists brought the practice to New York City. In the 1870s, a German immigrant named Martin Hildebrandt, who had tattooed both Union and Confederate troops during the Civil War, set up a tattoo shop on Oak Street, thought to be the first in the United States.

In 1891, Samuel O'Reilly, who years earlier had set up a tattoo shop in the Bowery, patented his electric "Tattoo Machine," which revolutionized tattooing overnight. Steve Gilbert notes that O'Reilly made a "small fortune" by tattooing and by selling his manufactured machine, inks, and designs. He also made private house calls for wealthier people who did not wish to venture into the Bowery, known for its cheap entertainment and squalor. In addition he was commissioned to tattoo circus people.[13]

Charles Wagner took over O'Reilly's studio when he died in 1908, patented his own machine, and continued to tattoo in the Bowery studio until his death in 1953. Wagner estimated that he tattooed tens of thousands of people during his career, including fifty "completely covered circus and sideshow attractions."[14]

A diagram of the original Samuel O'Reilly tattooing machine, which was patented on December 8, 1891

Charles Wagner (third from left) standing in front of the Bowery tattoo studio in 1910 after he took it over from O'Reilly

The practice of displaying tattooed people originated in Europe. Centuries before Captain Cook displayed the Tahitian Omai, European seamen frequently captured or purchased tattooed individuals and put them on display at fairgrounds and markets in Europe. In 1560, for instance, a French seaman captured an Inuit family in Greenland and put them on display in France and Germany.[15]

The showman P. T. Barnum created the first U.S. exhibits of unusual people in Barnum's American Museum, which opened in New York in 1841. At his museum, Barnum featured James F. O'Connell, the first tattooed American to be put on exhibit. O'Connell had a story similar to that of many tattooed attractions. He claimed to have been captured by "savages" in Ponape, in the Caroline Islands, and tattooed forcibly by beautiful maidens. He performed in circuses and in vaudeville throughout the United States for twenty years.[16]

The transcontinental railroad, completed in 1869, brought circuses and their displays of tattooed people into communities across America. In many of the towns James O'Connell visited, residents had never seen tattoos before, and at times "women and children screamed with horror when they met him."[17]

When the tattoo machine brought faster, easier, and cheaper tattooing, some people—both men and women—had themselves tattooed in order to become circus attractions. Tattooed women began to appear in circuses in the 1880s.[18] One of the women, La Belle Irene, appeared in London claiming she was tattooed in Texas, at that time a "strange and savage land," as protection from "unwelcome advances from the natives."[19]

Other circuses, such as Ringling Brothers and Cole Brothers, began to compete with Barnum and Bailey, and sideshows became more extreme. They included tattooed people who were also sword swallowers, fire-eaters, strong men, fat ladies, or fortune-tellers. But after World War II, circus "freak" shows and exhibits of tattooed people became less common. Tattoos were no longer unusual, thanks to the booming tattoo businesses in major cities and ports such as Norfolk, Virginia, and Honolulu, where many U.S. servicemen stood in block-long lines to receive three-dollar tattoos.[20] In addition, enlightened attitudes toward physical disabilities made circus and carnival sideshows less appealing. Tattoo artists continued to tattoo at carnivals, however, moving from town to town with the show.

Betty Broadbent received full body tattoos in the 1920s from Charles Wagner and Joe Van Hart. She was employed by all the major sideshows of the time, including Ringling Bros. and Barnum and Bailey Circus. In 1981 she was the first person to be honored by the Tattoo Hall of Fame.

Betty Broadbent
Tattooed Lady

"A Deviant Practice in the Public Mind".................

The ready availability and low cost of tattooing; its association with circus sideshows, carnivals, and amusement arcades; and its prominence in seedy parts of cities resulted in a negative view of tattooing. By the mid-twentieth century, writes University of Connecticut sociology professor Clinton Sanders, "tattooing was firmly established as a . . . deviant practice in the public mind,"[21] sometimes with good reason.

Several years before his death in June 2001 at age eighty-two, tattoo artist Tom Breitweg, known as Tatts Tommy, described how he moved from town to town with a carnival. In an interview, Breitweg pointed out the lack of sanitation when he tattooed at a state fair in the 1960s: "The machine would go in a grip [suitcase], wrapped up—boom—there was no sterilization . . . . When they got to the new place, you would rinse them off and go to work, that was it. But of course, you didn't have what you got today. There was no cleanliness about it."[22]

Samuel Steward, an English professor who left teaching in 1952 and became a highly respected professional tattoo artist, described the environment of the Sportland Arcade on South State Street in Chicago during the 1950s and 1960s:

> The floor was a filthy mess of mud, sawdust, dried spittle, torn newspapers, and wine bottles here and there. The flash on the walls had [a] primitive look. The machines were powered by an old direct-current generator . . . the needles [were] filthy with such a gummy coating of old dried ink-spatters and grease that you were afraid to touch them.[23]

Concerned about health issues and the association of tattoo parlors with unsavory parts of town, city officials began to restrict or ban tattooing. An outbreak of hepatitis during the 1950s was allegedly connected to Coney Island tattoo artists who were suspected of working under unsanitary conditions.[24]

When tattooing was at its height, the Navy port of Norfolk, Virginia, had what tattoo artist Paul Franklin Rogers called "the greatest tattoo block of all

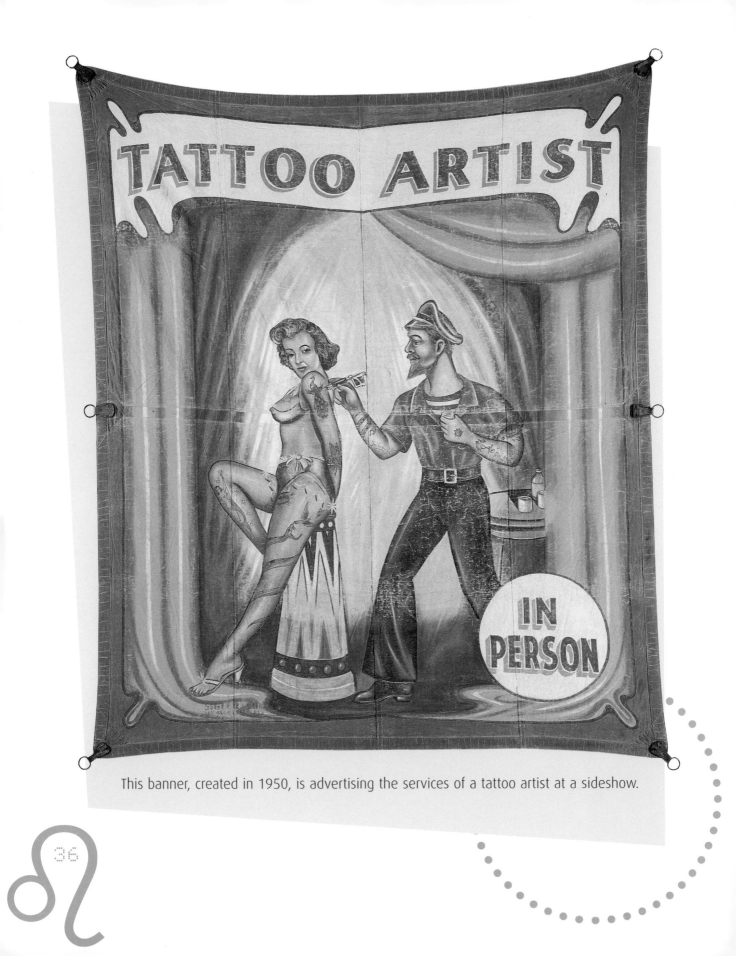

This banner, created in 1950, is advertising the services of a tattoo artist at a sideshow.

times," with eleven tattoo artists in one block and sixteen licensed artists in the city. Following World War II, Norfolk leaders worked to change the city's image as a "seedy port town," and in early 1950 health officials, worried about hepatitis, began to deny applications for new tattoo licenses. Norfolk officials outlawed tattooing altogether in May 1952.[25]

Modern Primitives and the Tattoo Renaissance

During the 1960s, American society changed rapidly and drastically. This was the time of the civil rights and women's rights movements and protests against the war in Vietnam. Many American youth wanted to change society and rebelled against the "establishment"—the traditional way of life. On school campuses across the United States, students who had once adhered to dress codes were going to class barefoot and wearing ripped jeans and love beads. In San Francisco, the 1967 "Summer of Love" included street theater, dancing, music, artistic events, body painting, and "happenings" in the famed Haight-Ashbury district, exemplifying the free spirit associated with the decade.

Tattoo artist Lyle Tuttle had been tattooing in San Francisco since 1952, but the counterculture made Tuttle's shop "the tattoo center of the San Francisco hippie movement," according to the late Arnold Rubin, history professor at University of California Los Angeles.[26] Among Tuttle's customers were several women who were notable for acquiring tattoos at a time when the practice was not only questionable but a predominantly male activity. In 1970, blues singer Janis Joplin, the "first rock star of the counterculture," hosted a party in which "everyone was going to have to submit to the needle of her friend Lyle Tuttle, whose work already decorated Janis's body in three places." [27] Other early customers of Tuttle include singer Joan Baez, singer and actress Cher, and actor Peter Fonda.

As tattooing regained prestige in the 1970s, artists with degrees in fine art were tattooing, and customers were educated professionals with money to spend for quality work. Tattoos were often large-scale custom designs. Both artists and customers looked to Japanese and tribal sources, such as those from indigenous cultures, and imagery from popular culture, such as science fiction and comic books, for inspiration, new techniques, and the use of color. Cliff Raven, who obtained a bachelor of arts in fine arts from Indiana University, and Ed Hardy, tattoo artist, publisher, and historian, are examples of artists who were part of a "tattoo renaissance" (or rebirth) as it has been called.[28]

Female tattoo artists have joined this elite group and include Ruth Marten, who trained at Boston's Museum School. In 1977, Marten tattooed a dolphin on the bicep of Pretenders' singer Chrissie Hynde.[29] Artist and former fashion designer Jill Jordan is known for tattooing a rosary on Cher's upper arm, and she has also tattooed members of the Indigo Girls.[30] Journalist Margo Mifflin believes that female tattoo artists have brought a new sensitivity to tattoo placement on female customers, creating designs that complement the female body.[31]

Popularity of Body Piercing

Like tattooing, body piercing of the ear, navel, or nipple has been practiced for millennia by men, women, and children in many different cultures, including prehistoric clans; ancient Egyptians, Roman soldiers, and Greek and Roman philosophers; and Native American, Asian, African, and other indigenous groups. Piercing was popular in Europe until the first half of the 1900s. Then two world wars overshadowed body-piercing fashions, and the practice seemed to disappear or at least was not widely apparent.

Piercings on different parts of the face became a popular extension of the multiple piercings that crept up along the ears throughout the 1980s.

Nevertheless, military personnel, following a long tradition, continued to have body piercings. American sailors, for example, customarily had an ear pierced as part of rituals to mark the crossing of the equator.[32] Sailors also believed in the common superstition that ear piercing improves vision. Skippers pierced the ear on the side opposite to that used on the telescope, and other sailors had both ears pierced, believing this would improve their sight while on watch. [33]

During the 1970s, artists, musicians, and fashion designers again resurrected body piercing in Europe and the United States. Through the 1980s and 1990s, body piercing became part of the American mainstream culture. Teenage girls and women began to have their ears double- or triple-pierced—or more—and to have the cartilage of the upper ear pierced. Nose, tongue, and navel piercings also became popular.

When homosexual men began wearing an earring during the 1970s to signify gay pride or to identify themselves, they placed one earring in the right ear in accordance with their motto: "left is right; right is wrong." This meant wearing an earring in the left ear indicated a person was straight; an earring in the right ear could be a sign a person was gay. The earring became a symbol of homosexuality and added to the stereotypes of homosexual men as effeminate. But by the 1990s, the public began to reject the stereotypes associated with men's ear piercings and teenage boys and men had first one, and then both ears pierced. Sociology professor Clinton Sanders commemorated the receipt of his Ph.D. by piercing his left ear.[34] Recently actor Harrison Ford celebrated his fifty-fifth birthday the same way.

In an article in the *Chronicle of Higher Education*, Karla Haworth reports that national statistics are hard to come by, but "doctors and clinicians at college health centers say they are seeing more 'body art'—tattoos, piercing, branding, and even sewing of the skin—than ever before. What was fringe in the early 1990s is now mainstream."[35] In short, millions of Americans have or soon will have marked or modified their bodies in some way, probably with tattoos or piercings.

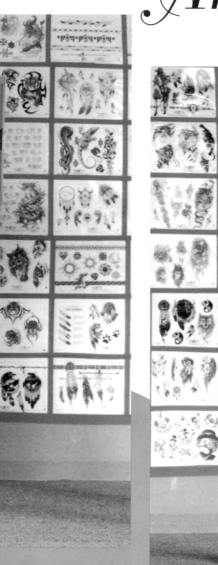

Art From

The hundreds of pieces of flash that line the walls at tattoo shops include many different categories of traditional and nontraditional tattoos.

Head to Toe

The increasing popularity of tattooing over the past few decades raises questions about whether contemporary tattoos have any connections with past practices. What do some of the diverse modern-day tattoos mean?

With so many types of designs available, how does a person distinguish one from another? In a tattoo shop or at a tattoo convention, where there are collections of flash and portfolios of photographs displaying tattoos, the designs are categorized by terms that are familiar to most tattoo artists and many customers across the United States.

Tribal Tattoos

In tattoo jargon, the designation *tribal* "encompasses native motifs from preindustrial cultures the world over."[1] Tribal tattoos are bold, abstract, and mostly solid black. An artist who specializes in tribal tattoos in his shop asserts on his Web site that the "widespread resurgence and acceptance" of tribal tattooing are prompted by the increasing "research on Tribal people, their arts, Tattoos, and lifestyles, and more and more available images of Tattooed people." In this artist's view, "Pretechnological designs (i.e., Black Tribal) give the wearer a link to the origins of all present human society, a past Tribal culture wherein the Tattoo had an inner meaning to the wearer, not just a modern symbol of our present culture such as a Mickey Mouse Tattoo."[2]

This tribal tattoo on subject Sharon Baker exhibits typical tribal qualities—it is bold, black, one-dimensional, and abstract. (tattoo artist Gordon Toi Hatfield from the book *Dedicated by Blood: The Meaning of Ta Moko*)

Tattoo artists working in and adapting tribal styles are some of the best known and highly respected artists today. Among them is Hawaiian Leo Zulueta, whose artistic style is extremely influential in the tattoo community. Other artists known for striking tribal designs are Cliff Raven, Alex Binnie, Trevor Marshall, and Jill Jordan, whose tribal adaptations enhance the female anatomy.

Art critic Victoria Lautman believes that tribal tattoos have become popu-lar because they are so different from traditional tattoo styles, a "counterpoint to the wildly colorful images that have been tattooing's mainstay since the 1960s." They also adapt to individual anatomy, "accentuating each body's own structure and contours."[3]

Ironically, the popularity of tribal tattooing among Westerners may have the effect of preserving indigenous tattoo styles. The governments of some countries, such as Borneo, consider tattoos a holdover of an old-fashioned, traditional society, and actively discourage them. Leo Zulueta notes that "those traditions are dying out where they originated; the original peoples have no interest in preserving them—they'd rather have a ghetto blaster and a Jeep and a pack of Marlboro cigarettes. The Western encroachment has triumphed."[4]

"Old School" Tattoos

Before the tattoo renaissance of the late 1960s, tattoos in the United States and western Europe frequently were traditional designs, now called *old school* tattoos. Many of these designs have been popular for decades, such as ships, eagles, anchors, and panthers. Other types are associated with convicts, gangs, or white supremacist groups, sometimes all at once.

The standard images did not change much from the time the tattoo machine was invented in 1891 to the tattoo renaissance of the 1960s. Anthropologist Margo DeMello writes that "the classic American tattoo . . . is a literal tattoo: one whose meaning is readily understood and agreed to by members of the community."[5] They were in visible locations on the body, executed in bold colors and lines, and included words, such as the initials of the wearer, "Death Before Dishonor," or "USMC" (for United States Marine Corps), which made the meaning of the tattoo even easier to understand.[6]

Old school tattoos are often associated with the military and include the traditional navy tattoos: ships, anchors, hula girls, mermaids, dragons, bluebirds, and eagles. John Kinlein, a 2000 graduate of the Maine Maritime Academy, had a traditional emblem of the Merchant Marine, a snake entwined around an anchor with the words "Don't Tread on Me," tattooed on his bicep.[7] One traditional tattoo design called "Man's Ruin" includes many of the elements suspected of contributing to a man's downfall: a cocktail glass, dice, playing cards, musical notes, or a seductive woman.[8]

43

A revival of interest in old school tattooing has led some tattoo artists to experiment with what is called "retro old-school" or "neo-traditional" style. They offer bluebirds, anchors, "Man's Ruin," thorn-wrapped "sacred hearts" with flames, pinup girls, and other traditional images, using new techniques and colors, and creating a larger-than-life effect.[9]

Devotional or Memorial Tattoos

Like old school tattoos, devotional tattoos have a long history and are still popular today. Probably the most familiar form of the devotional tattoo is the heart inscribed with "I Love Mom." Names and initials to memorialize or to show devotion are also popular.

Some people choose to honor loved or admired individuals with portraits—whether the loved one is a spouse, a child, Elvis Presley, or a beloved Labrador retriever. Portraits are usually done in fine-line technique, which is executed with a single needle in a realistic manner.

Many tattoo artists discourage customers from having the names of sweethearts tattooed on their bodies. Some even feel that it is unlucky and can jinx the relationship. If a relationship ends, the person with the tattoo undoubtedly views it in a different light. Some people have the tattoo removed, covered up, or altered.

Other tattoos commemorate connections with loved ones in more subtle ways. A University of Maine student had a pumpkin tattooed over his heart to represent his pet name for his daughter. To demonstrate their intergenerational affection, a granddaughter, mother, and grandmother were all tattooed with the same design of violets, which traditionally symbolize memory.

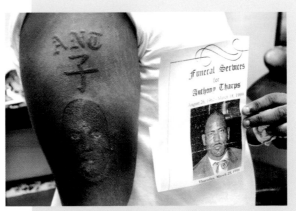

This memorial tattoo of a man's deceased father displays the father's initials at top and his portrait below.

Amy Krakow described the best devotional tattoo she had seen, on a "rock and roller from Brooklyn." One morning after the man's girlfriend put on her lipstick, she kissed him on the neck. "It looked so good," the man said, "that I went off to my tattooist and had him tattoo a red kiss, right where she had kissed me."[10]

Prison Tattooing

Tattooing is universally forbidden in prisons, but is pervasive among inmates. Jailed tattooists manage to decorate their fellow inmates in ingenious ways, which is an "embarrassment" to corrections officials.[11] As Richard Stratton, ex-convict and editor of *Prison Life*, points out, "one does not go to prison for obeying the rules."[12]

Prisoners make tattoo machines out of electric shavers, needles out of guitar strings, and ink reservoirs from the barrels of ballpoint pens. They obtain ink from pens, the prison printshop, newspapers soaked to release the ink, or mixing ash from scorched shoe rubber with water or urine. Flash and stencils are not available, so artists work freehand.

Douglas Kent Hall, who photographed tattooed bodybuilders in New Mexico and California prisons, notes that "this world, which offers so much idle time, so little challenge, and no real hope, inspires convicts to choose any possible means of expressing themselves. They use their bodies like a canvas, a confessional, an instrument of private communication. In order to establish the identity necessary to survive, they tag themselves with tattoos."[13] A convict, Jerry, expresses the sentiment a little differently: "[T]his is my body. It's my novel, man, my poem, and I'm just gonna keep writin' on it."[14]

The marijuana leaf, the number 13, the thirteenth letter of the alphabet, "M" (which stands for marijuana) are popular among all inmates, as are birds, symbolizing freedom or power, skulls and other figures of death, spiders and webs, roses, snakes, and religious images.[15] Teardrops at the corners of the eyes represent time spent in prison, murders committed, or the death of fellow gang members.[16]

Gang tattooing and prison tattooing are often impossible to tell apart, since some gang members end up in prison and many gangs persist behind prison bars. The first tattoo a gang member gets may be self-administered or done by a nonprofessional and badly rendered. It may consist of standard street symbols, such as gang names ("Bloods," "Crips," "VL," or "Vice Lords"); 187 (the section of California's criminal code for homicide); or 666 (the mark of Satan). Members of Hispanic gangs have adopted images of bleeding daggers, lowrider cars, or "cholo" or "pachuco," tough-guy characters with drooping mustaches and sombreros pulled over their faces.[17]

Racist prison and gang tattoos reflect imagery of the Aryan Brotherhood, a prison gang formed at San Quentin in the 1960s. Their characteristic tattoos include the words "white power" (or some variation), the initials "A.Y.M" for Aryan Youth Movement, "A.B." for Aryan Brotherhood, Nazi swastikas, and the word "Germany."[18] White supremacist tattoos also include Celtic designs such as the Celtic Cross to indicate white northern European ancestry.[19]

This Culver City gang member proudly wears his gang name across his stomach near a variety of other personal tattoos.

Not all people with gang- or prison-related tattoo images are gang members or ex-convicts, however. In fact, ex-convict Stratton notes that "even primitive jailhouse tattoos are now copied by freeworld tattooists,"[20] and Hall's book, *Prison Tattoos*, comes with a page of temporary tattoos based on those of the men he photographed. In addition, many people may not realize they are getting a so-called jailhouse tattoo. Canadian tattoo artist and professor of medical illustration Steve Gilbert recalls that he was fourteen when he had "a little number 13" tattooed on his leg.[21]

Some people unintentionally get a tattoo with connections to prison life—a Celtic tattoo, for example—simply because they like the design. Celtic arts in general have experienced a resurgence of popularity in recent years, and tattoo artists have joined the trend by creating flash sheets with Celtic tattoos or by specializing in Celtic designs. However, since white supremacist groups sometimes mark themselves with Celtic tattoos, it's become important to explore the meaning of these designs before having them permanently marked on one's skin.

Japanese Influence

Over the centuries, the privileged and royalty in Western societies have sought the services of highly skilled Japanese tattoo artists. For example, in 1882 when the Duke of Clarence and the Duke of York (later King George V) of England were teenagers, they visited Japan with their tutor, and abiding by their father's wishes, were tattooed by a well-known Japanese tattoo master.[22]

Tattooing, called *irezumi* ("to insert"), has a long history in Japan and flourished during the eighteenth century, influenced by the tradition of woodblock printing—printing from inked designs carved into wooden blocks. However, a repressive government dictated what it deemed cultural excesses, banned various types of art and theater, and established dress codes. Because colorful kimonos (robes) were outlawed, the Japanese replaced them with elaborate tattoos, designs that covered the back and extended to the upper legs and arms and the sides of the chest, appearing like a kimono or body suit.[23]

Japanese tattoo artists have inspired diverse Western tattoo artists, including British "King of the Tattooists" George Burchett, Sailor Jerry Collins of Honolulu, and one of today's most highly respected tattoo artists, Don Ed Hardy.

Three Japanese men show off traditional colorful tattoos that were influenced by their heritage.

In 1970, Japan's master tattoo artist, Kazuo Oguri, began to correspond with Honolulu artist Sailor Jerry Collins; the two eventually met in Honolulu in 1972. The following year Oguri traveled to the west coast of the United States, "where he demonstrated tattooing by hand and exchanged designs and tattoo information" with U.S. tattoo artists. He also attended the first tattoo convention held in Houston, Texas, in 1975.[24] Oguri's influence has "trickled down" to many U.S. tattoo artists and has helped promote the Japanese art of tattooing.

Tattoo artist Steve Gilbert, for instance, currently tattoos in the four-hundred-year-old Japanese method of *tebori*, using an instrument with needles attached to a bamboo handle. Gilbert dips the needles of the bamboo instrument into ink, then presses the needles rapidly and rhythmically into the customer's skin.[25]

Comic Book and Fantasy Characters ....

Comic book characters have been popular tattoo subjects for several decades. While Popeye and Betty Boop adorned sailors in the early twentieth century, one of the most popular tattoo images in the military is now the Warner Brothers cartoon character, the Tasmanian Devil, or Taz. He sometimes appears as a soldier or sailor, swings an anchor, or brandishes an M-16.[26] Other popular tattoos include Batman, Winnie the Pooh characters, and the more "adult" images of artists R. Crumb, Coop, and fantasy comics and illustrations like those of Frank Frazetta and H. R. Giger.

Cartoon images appeal to many people, including celebrities. Whoopi Goldberg is tattooed with the bird Woodstock from the "Peanuts" comic strip; Mark Wahlberg sports Sylvester the Cat and Tweety Bird on his ankle; Janet Jackson wears Mickey and Minnie Mouse; Tony Danza displays on his bicep R. Crumb's Mr. Natural doing his "Keep on Truckin'" step; and Jon Bon Jovi has a Superman logo.

Custom Tattoos ....

Some tattoo artists work primarily from flash; some do exclusively custom work. Many artists do both. Typically, ideas for a custom design come from tattoo books and magazines, books on art, needlework, and natural history, and many other publications. Maine tattoo artist Ed "Wiz" Dumont, working on designs for two custom tattoos, found pictures to use as models for one design in a book on the restoration of Michelangelo's paintings for the Sistine Chapel ceiling, and for another design in a book about the nesting habits of eagles. New Hampshire artist Juli Moon created a tattooed "gold and garnet" bracelet for a customer from photos of artifacts found in a Viking archaeological site.

Other tattoo artists have created custom designs from artwork done by the customer. Tattoo artist Trevor Marshall, who works in New Hampshire and New Zealand, tattooed a loon designed by his customer, an artist who had worked on the design for several years.

49

At the Mad Hatter's Tea Party, a convention for tattoo enthusiasts in Maine, a woman shows off a cusom tattoo design on her arm while her son wears a temporary tattoo.

There are few rules for custom designs, except that both artist and customer should have an understanding of what the final design should look like, what colors will be used, where it will be located on the body, and what the cost will be. Many tattoo artists charge $100 to $200 and up per hour for custom work and are booked for months in advance. Some provide an estimate before beginning the design, and others work on a large design over a period of time and allow the customer to pay as the work is completed.

Temporary Tattoos

Temporary tattoos, as the term suggests, can be removed. They are popular with young people and adults who do not want to permanently mark their bodies. These tattoos are usually mounted on paper and transferred to the skin by wetting the backing with a damp sponge and pressing firmly. After about thirty seconds, the paper is peeled off, leaving a design that can be removed with rubbing alcohol.

Although temporary tattoos would seem to be an innocent indulgence, their popularity may have grown because of a 1980s urban legend—a popular story that appears suddenly, is false or contains only a grain of truth, spreads quickly, and frequently relates an incident that happened to a "friend of a friend." The legend claimed that certain types of temporary tattoos were impregnated with the mind-altering substance LSD.[27]

Temporary tattoos are now available in a wide variety of stores, ranging from minimarts to chic boutiques. Children give them to one another as birthday party favors, and adults wear them with Halloween costumes, to startle family members, or to "try out" the idea of having a real tattoo.

Rings and

Piercings and tattoos in the Western world were once associated with countercultures such as the punk scene; yet, these types of body alterations are now becoming more accepted into mainstream society.

Things

hroughout history, people have pierced their skin to insert pieces of "metal, bone, shell, ivory or glass to wear as an ornament,"[1] or to show social status. For example, among the Tlingit, indigenous people of southeast Alaska, ear piercing was directly related to a person's place in society. Social position was determined by the wealth of the family into which the individual was born. Although a Tlingit could rarely better his own social standing, he could raise the station of his sister's children and his grandchildren by "potlatching," or hosting a community feast. At a potlatch the host paid a member of his moiety (group) to pierce the rims of the children's ears. At additional potlatches, other holes were added. A great amount of wealth was required to host the feast and pay the person to pierce the children's ears. Consequently, the resulting series of holes marked an individual as a member of the nobility.[2]

Today, most piercings practiced in piercing and tattooing studios are of the common ear and navel variety. Some people pierce themselves or have friends do the job. But for safety and health reasons, piercings should not be attempted by amateurs—self-piercing is highly risky behavior. The type of piercings associated with the counterculture can be especially dangerous for the inexperienced.

From Counterculture
......Into the Mainstream

Body piercing in Western culture was first associated with SM, or sado-masochistic relationships (persons inflicting pain and being subjected to pain for pleasure), and the modern primitive, or urban primitive, movement. Fakir Musafar, who calls himself a shaman, has been dubbed the father of the modern primitive movement. He coined the term in 1967 "to describe a . . . person who responds to primal urges and does something with the body."[3] In brief, modern primitives believe that Western society's technology and industrialization have numbed the senses. They have revived various types of body piercing, scarification, and other modifications to encourage spiritual exploration and personal expression.

Born in Aberdeen, South Dakota, in 1930, Fakir Musafar was named Roland Loomis. Early in his childhood, he was influenced by carnival sideshows and articles in *National Geographic* and encyclopedias about people from other cultures.[4] As an adult, he adopted his new name from a fakir of nineteenth-century India. Fakirs were Sufi (mystical Muslim) or Hindu holy men who "possessed miraculous powers, such as the ability to walk on fire"[5] and to perform other feats of "endurance, self-torture, and 'magic.'"[6]

Carnivals of the 1930s included body piercers and "fakirs" such as Krinko of Krinko's Great Combined Carnival Side Shows. When he was a child in India, Krinko had his tongue pierced by his father. Krinko repeatedly worked a rope through the hole in his tongue to toughen it and keep it from healing. He was eventually able to pull a cart with a rope inserted through the hole in his tongue. In the sideshow, Krinko invited members of the audience to drive a nail through his tongue. Because the hole was invisible to the audience, Krinko was able to position a nail in it and give the impression that someone was pounding it through his tongue.[7]

During the 1970s and 1980s, punk rock performers and their followers linked cutting and piercing the skin to youth culture. Beginning with an August 29, 1969, performance, Detroit punk rocker Iggy Pop cut himself with drumsticks and with broken glass. Other punk entertainers made "self injury" part of their acts, and punks adopted "anti-fashion gestures of tattooing, body piercing, and self-laceration such as carving profane words into one's skin."[8]

54

This Malaysian fakir in 1938 has his flesh pierced with needles while weights hang from hooks in his chest.

Body piercing eventually moved from the youth culture into the mainstream—at least in some of its less extreme forms. Although anything inserted into a perforation in the body for decorative or ritual purposes qualifies as body piercing, certain types of piercings are more acceptable to mainstream society and culture than others.

........Who Pierces What and How

There is a big difference between who practices body piercing and who is qualified to practice it. Before professional ear piercing was widely available it was common for people to receive their first body piercing from a friend armed with an ice cube, a cork, and a needle. With this type of do-it-yourself ear piercing, underage young people could avoid getting parental consent. In fact, it became so widespread among teenagers that the practice was depicted in the 1998 remake of the Disney film *The Parent Trap*.

Many people visit a jewelry kiosk in a mall to have their earlobes, ear cartilage, or other body parts pierced with a piercing gun. The bright lights and friendly atmosphere of the mall lead customers (including teenagers and their parents) to believe that the jewelry kiosk must be a safer place than the piercing studio with its multitattooed, metal-intensive staff.

The truth is that ear-piercing guns can never be properly sterilized. Their needles can be new each time or placed in autoclave machines—standard equipment in doctors' offices and hospitals for sterilizing instruments—but the gun itself cannot be sterilized. Also, the guns pierce by blunt force, traumatizing flesh and damaging cartilage.[9] Only professional body piercers should perform any type of body piercing, even of earlobes.

Some people get piercings because they are curative, usually in the spiritual sense of channeling energy or healing past wounds.[10] Others want to have piercing performed as part of a ceremony, to shock or rebel, or simply because they like the way the piercing looks.

Since the early 1990s, when fashion models on runways and in advertisements began to wear navel rings, body piercing has become increasingly fashionable and aesthetic rather than an act of deep personal significance. Fake navel and nose rings for the unpierced, like temporary tattoos, are examples of the fashionable approach to body art; they provide the look without having to experience pain or permanence.

What Is That Called? ·

There are several dozen names for piercings, most of which are consistent within body art culture. Some of the names are obvious because they refer to the body parts that are pierced, such as the nostril, tongue, or earlobe. Other names include:

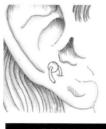

ANTITRAGUS

Antitragus: Pierces the point of ear cartilage opposite the tragus. Most people wear a ring in this piercing; some wear a barbell.

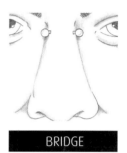

BRIDGE

Bridge: Pierces the bridge of the nose, between the eyes. Most people wear a barbell with beads on each end in a bridge piercing.

Conch: Pierces ridge of cartilage within the concave innermost part of the ear. Most people wear a barbell or a ring in this piercing.

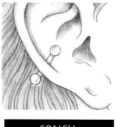

CONCH

Daith: Pierces the inner curve of the ear closest to the side of the face, above the tragus. Most people wear a ring in this piercing.

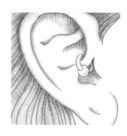

DAITH

Ear Project: The combined artistic effect of several ear piercings, often including an industrial.

Industrial: A single piece of jewelry, often a very long barbell, that extends through two piercings in the ear, one in the front and the other in the back, so that the body of the barbell extends across the inside of the ear.

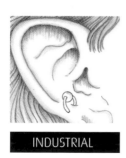

INDUSTRIAL

Labret: A piercing about midway below the lower lip and above the chin. Jewelry is usually a barbell with

LABRET

a flat piece on the inside of the lip and a ball, spike, or other adornment on the outside.

Madison: A surface-to-surface piercing at the base of the throat. When jewelry—usually a barbell—is worn in the Madison, this piercing resembles the pendant on a necklace.

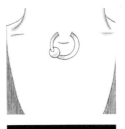

Orbit: A piercing consisting of two holes in a single surface of the ear (for example, the earlobe or upper cartilage) with a ring worn through both holes.

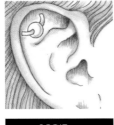

ORBIT

Rook: A piercing that goes through the top ridge of cartilage on the inside of the ear, usually done with a ring.

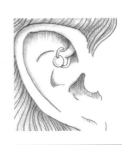

ROOK

Septum: A piercing through the partition between the nostrils. Jewelry can be rings or "tusks."

Tragus: Pierces the small point of cartilage at the front of the ear, closest to the face and next to the hinge of the jaw. Tragus piercings accommodate a variety of jewelry, most often rings, barbells, or curved barbells.

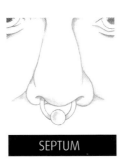

SEPTUM

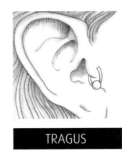

TRAGUS

Jewelry

Body piercing jewelry is quite different from the costume jewelry found at the local boutique or mall kiosk. It is made specifically for body piercing by companies that specialize in this area, such as Anatometal or Gauntlet. To be safe for initial body piercings, jewelry must be made of implant-grade surgical steel, titanium, or niobium. Surgical steel is always silver in color, but titanium and

niobium come in colors. Gold can be used in healed piercings. Standard types of jewelry include:

- **Captive bead ring (CBR)**: A ring with a break in which a bead is inserted and held in place by tension. While the rings must be made of implant-grade surgical steel, niobium, or titanium, the bead can be made of those metals or almost any kind of precious or semiprecious gem.

- **Barbell**: A straight piece of metal with balls that screw on both ends.

- **Circular barbell**: A barbell curved in a semicircular shape, with balls screwed on each end.

A tattoo and piercing artist displays a case of piercing accessories, including captive bead rings, barbells, and plugs.

- **Plug**: A cylindrical, solid piercing used in stretched earlobes, for example.
- **Nostril screw**: A stud for the nostril with a spiraled post that goes inside the nose to keep it from falling out.

The thickness of jewelry is indicated by gauge. The higher the gauge, the smaller the jewelry. The lowest number, 00, is the thickest piece of jewelry made. A gauge of 20 is usually the thinnest. The thinner gauges are sometimes called "cheese cutter" jewelry because thin wire can cut or the body can reject the piercing.

A College Student's Piercing Experience

In January 1999, Pennsylvania State University journalism student James Conroy began writing a series of stories called "James' Adventures in Piercing." The series included one article on henna, but most were on piercings, and were published in Penn State's newspaper, the *Daily Collegian*.

Every week, Conroy had a different part of his body pierced at one of the college town's piercing studios. He recorded his experiences for posterity and for "the good of mankind." He also provided "consumer reports" of sorts for his readers, listing prices for the piercings at various local studios, describing the experience, what kind of preparation was necessary, what the piercing felt like, the aftercare, his friends' reactions, and in a recap article, the fate of his nine piercings.

Some of Conroy's piercings were successful, and others were not. At the end of ten weeks, only five of his piercings remained: tongue, nipple, nostril, orbital, and genital. His eyebrow ring fell out in the shower, and he removed his labret before his parents, who knew nothing about his piercings, came for a visit. He removed the tragus piercing because it annoyed him, and the navel ring fell out while he was playing basketball.

As a new piercee, Conroy shares experiences the uninitiated might not have thought about. For his tongue piercing, Conroy had to stick his tongue out as far as possible so that it could be held with a clamp that looks like a "medieval torture device." The next day, Conroy says, "it took me about an hour to eat a bowl of ravioli." Meanwhile, the labret caused a wave of nausea, and it cost him fifty dollars "to get sick in a strange place and have a steel rod thrust through my lip." The tragus pierce "feels really strange" because "there's a piece of metal sticking through that little thing that protrudes from your ear."

For those considering navel piercing, Conroy advises, "save yourself from embarrassment, clean out the belly button lint before you go." About the nipple ring, Conroy warns, "If you're thinking of getting your nipple pierced—stop. Think about it again and if you still want it done, at least I warned you."[11]

For his series of articles, Conroy was awarded the best college newspaper column of the year from the Pennsylvania Newspaper Association. The series was also posted on the Internet.

This
carved
wooden
head
represents
a Maori man
that is
recognized by his
distinctive patterns
of moko. These carvings were a sign
of great courage and regarded as
revealing a man's true identity.

Scarification

A scar is defined as "a mark on the body after a surface injury heals," which seems benign enough. After all, countless people show off their "battle scars" while telling elaborate tales about injuries or surgeries. Even a president took part in this type of show-and-tell. When President Lyndon B. Johnson (1963–1969) told reporters about his successful operation to remove his gallbladder, he both shocked and amused the press by picking up his shirt and pointing to his scar.

Yet the word also has a sinister connotation, as was evident in *Scarface*, a classic 1930s gangster film; the gangster's scarred face instantly suggests that he's a menace. A scar can also refer to a trauma—a tragic accident, a death, or other life event that leaves an indelible imprint, or psychological scar, on a person. In addition, the word is a metaphor for environmental destruction—pristine land is often scarred by mining, logging, road and dam building, and other industrial activities.

So what does it mean when someone voluntarily has a scar produced on his or her body? Is this a negative appraisal or proud assessment of self? An attention-getting device? The result of a psychological illness?

What Is Scarification?

Scarification, like extreme body piercing, is frequently associated with counterculture or alternative lifestyles, such as those in SM relationships and the modern primitive movement. But since the late 1980s, scarification has become increasingly popular across the United States and Canada. It has moved out of the subculture and is practiced in numerous tattoo and body piercing studios. Nevertheless, it's not for the faint-hearted. Why? Because it involves branding—burning the skin, usually with hot metal—or cutting the skin. Both activities can be painful, and after healing both create scars, a process known as cicatrization. The terms scarification and cicatrization are often used interchangeably.

Not all scars are flat on the skin. Some form keloids—excessive growth of fibrous tissues that create a thick scar that rises above the skin surface. Keloids are more likely to form on dark-skinned people than on those with light skin. In some cases, ashes, clay, ink, or other material may be rubbed into a cut to form sharply elevated keloids.

Skin type, whether it's thin or dense, also determines how scars will form. The healing process plays a role as well. Some people remove their scabs and repeat their cuts in order to develop a more visible scar. Because no person's body is exactly like another's, the scar that forms will have its own unique characteristics.

Cutting: From Ancient to Modern Practices

For thousands of years people have cut their bodies to produce scars, usually as part of religious or rite-of-passage rituals. Scarring was a widespread practice among the indigenous people of New Zealand and Australia, for example. Maori men of New Zealand covered their faces with tattoo markings that were actually carvings and would be called ink rubbings today. A Maori artist of moko (carving of the face) sketched a design on a man's skin and then used a bone chisel to cut into the skin similar to the way woodcarvings are made. "Ink would be placed in the cuts to create the tattoo. The process could take days or weeks depending on the individual's tolerance for pain."[1]

Scarring was common among the indigenous aborigines of Australia, but it is "now restricted almost entirely to parts of Arnhem Land. Scarring is like a language inscribed on the body, where each deliberately placed scar tells a story of pain, endurance, identity, status, beauty, courage, sorrow or grief."[2]

A body art exhibit traveling through Australia in 2000 and 2001 explained that a practice of the past required "Wardaman people [to] have two cuts on each shoulder, two on the chest and four on the belly. Jawoyn people only have one cut on the shoulder, one on the chest and a big long one on the belly. Other people have three cuts on the shoulder and many on the belly." The cutting ritual took place when young people turned sixteen or seventeen years of age. Without the scars a person could not take part in ceremonial events, including marriages and burials. A sharp stone made the cuts and burned wood or ash placed on the wound stopped the bleeding and promoted healing.[3]

In Papua New Guinea, it was common to initiate girls at puberty with markings on the abdomen. The first menstrual period was a time for cuttings under the breasts and on the back. After a woman's first child was born, final markings were made on the back, neck, buttocks, arms, and legs. [4]

Scars also show family heritage, membership in a particular community, and social class. For Ben Lewis, a healer in Papua New Guinea, "the ceremonies and the initiation scars, or marks, were part of my induction into manhood and training in the ways of Sharmanic [Shamanic] healing and medicine." He wears "the marks of the ancestral crocodile. This is a power mark, a spirit, a security used for protection and connection with the totems and ancestors of my clan, the 'Crocodile Men of East Sepik,' Yenchen Village." He explained:

> In the middle Sepik region, it is believed that migrating ancestral crocodiles established human populations. During the wagan initiation ceremony, which celebrates the return of the ancestral crocodile, young men from this region are initiated into manhood. The skin on the chest, back and buttocks of the initiate is cut with a bamboo sliver to test their physical strength and self-discipline. The scars, when healed, represent the teeth marks of the crocodile that has swallowed the initiates who are reborn as crocodile-men.[5]

Among the Yoruba in Nigeria, Africa, body scarification is an art form and ritual based on a proverb that says, "Open your hand, here are lines." The lines provide "visual identification and signify political allegiances or biographical facts regarding a person. Women have the most designs placed onto their bodies. The most common scarification sites are the face, neck, chest, abdomen, back, arms, back of hands, calf or lower leg and thighs."[6]

A woman in Nigeria wears a variety of traditional facial scars.

Scarification is practiced in many other African countries as well. Yombe women of Zaire were marked with crosshatch scars over most of their bodies. This indicated their high status and identified their culture. For the Bini, or people of Benin, scarification has served another purpose. According to Bini belief, the process heals or purifies the body. It has also been a way to indicate that girls and boys have become adults. In addition, scarification has symbolized marital commitment.

Creating scars is a skill passed from one Bini family member to another. The practitioner, called an *osiwu*, "uses a special knife to cut the patterns into the skin. To help darken the scar, a medication made of palm oil, soot, and a burnt tree root was applied as the wounds healed." Scar marks "are still important signs of beauty, heritage, and Bini citizenship." But today's young people are not as apt to be scarred. Instead they might wear clothes that have special scarification designs.[7]

Among the Luba of central Africa "scarification patterns and their meanings vary from region to region," but some marks impart an enduring message. For example, "Impolo are marks beneath the eyes to add cheerfulness to the smile . . . Nkaka is a pattern of triangles across the chest symbolizing the Luba belief that women contain and guard spiritual knowledge that men, especially Luba officials, must obey."[8]

During initiation ceremonies the Makonde of Mozambique carve chevrons (inverted Vs) into the faces of both girls and boys to identify their culture and indicate they have become adults. In the Rift and Omo valleys of southern Ethiopia, where numerous indigenous groups are located, men are scarred to show they have killed an enemy.

Similar rituals have been performed among the Kayapo of the southern Amazon basin. In the Kayapo ritual, it was a common practice to carve a large V on the chest "extending from shoulders to navel."[9]

The scarification on this Karo woman of Ethiopia is a sign of beauty that illustrates her strength and resistance to disease.

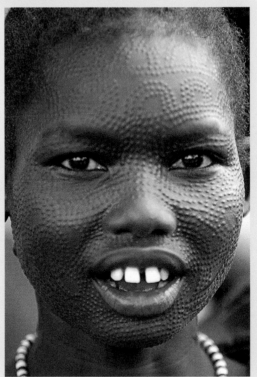

The Dinka females of Sudan cut their skin and create very intricate scar patterns to decorate their faces and upper body.

The scarification practices of indigenous groups in various parts of the world have prompted some Americans and Europeans today to mark their bodies in a similar fashion. While it's not unusual for people to cut themselves to create their scars, the more cautious have sought out artists with cutting expertise. Usually practitioners use a surgical scalpel or laser, cutting into the skin about 1/16 inch (2 mm). They may add tattoo ink, black ash, or other material so a keloid will develop.

What types of designs are created? They vary greatly, ranging from simple parallel lines, such as those used by native people, to intricate designs created by an artist or the person being cut. For example, a cutting design could look like a collar and tie on a man's chest, or the design could be connecting spirals covering a person's entire back.

In the body-art community today, scarification is considered a "natural" way to decorate the skin because it stems from prehistoric times. Although scarification can sometimes be one of the most dangerous forms of skin modification, those who mark their bodies in this manner are taking part in rituals—individual and group rites of passage—that to them have profound meanings and are part of their attempts to demonstrate who they are. This is especially true of those who are branded, which is another form of scarification.

Branding

The practice of branding to create scars certainly is not new. Since ancient times, branding has been a way to show proof of slave and livestock ownership. Criminals and army deserters in many parts of the world were branded as a form of punishment or for identification. In addition, branding has been and still is a rite of passage in many cultures; a brand marks a special life event such as coming of age, a wedding, or a birth.

Branding may also be a ceremonial event, an initiation into a hate group, gang, or an alternative community, for example. Members of music groups sometimes are branded to show their kinship. Branding is also popular on college campuses. Although branding is not sanctioned by Greek fraternity and sorority organizations, the practice has a long tradition among black fraternity brothers. Some have chosen slave designs to symbolize connections with their ancestors. More commonly, brands are fraternity letters. In addition, an increasing number of sorority sisters have taken part in branding rituals.

Among athletes, famous basketball star Michael Jordan has a fraternity brand on his chest. Other professional ballplayers have Omega Psi Phi or Kappa Alpha Psi brands seared on their arms, calves, thighs, or backsides.

How is a person branded? In some cases, people brand themselves or have friends do the job, although this is not recommended by professional branding artists. On occasion, amateurs experiment with dry ice, which burns the skin. For the most part, though, amateurs use whatever metal objects happen to be at hand and can be shaped into designs—paper clips, coat hangers, needles, cans, or screws. Horseshoes are common branding tools among fraternities, according to the Texas Tech Health Sciences Center.[10]

A fraternity brand of the Greek letters alpha phi alpha

Several years ago, a *Washington Post* reporter described a branding ritual that took place at Howard University:

> Imagine a carefully fashioned coat hanger, slow-roasted over blue-green flame of a Magic Chef range, heading for the fleshy expanse of your upper arm, your chest or the side of your behind. For a fraction of a second, you can feel the heat before it touches your skin. Your heart races and instinctively you want to draw back. But you don't. Because you want your brand to be sweet. Or if you think you'll move, you brace yourself, holding onto a sink or table; or perhaps you get somebody else to hold you down.
>
> Then comes the "hit," a quick "Psssssssst." Or maybe it's a "crackle" or "pop," not unlike the sound of Rice Krispies soaking in a bowl of milk. They say it doesn't really hurt. But the smell of burning flesh can be weird. Especially when it's yours.[11]

In a commercial studio, the process usually begins with a small bar of surgical steel that is heated until it is glowing orange, 1100°F (593°C). In some cases, a branding artist uses silver objects, ceramic pieces, or metal items like bolts and screws to create scar designs. A cautery pen, usually used for med-

A branding practitioner uses a metal branding bar to create a decorative design on his customer's back.

ical purposes such as removing abnormal skin tissue, is also used for branding, especially when designs are intricate or placed on a sensitive part of the body.

Whatever the branding implement, it is pressed onto a person's arm, back, shoulder, buttocks, thigh, ankle, or other part of the body, producing a third-degree burn. Each hit of hot metal, called a strike, must be precise and held on the skin for only one or two seconds. The strike is accompanied by a small puff of smoke and the smell of burning flesh. For a second there could be searing pain, but the nerves are destroyed so the pain does not last. In fact, some people who are branded say that the pain causes an "endorphin rush"— that is, the brain is numbed for a time, rather like the effects of an anesthetic or powerful pain reliever.

Usually a branding practitioner makes several strikes with a branding bar, and may use varied shapes and sizes to create a design. These are placed far enough apart to allow room for the scar to spread. After the burn heals, the scar will be two to four times larger than the width of the metal bar (or other object) that created the burn.

SIV or Scarification?.........................

In spite of the constant warnings that branding or cutting oneself is a dangerous form of body marking, countless individuals who practice scarification produce their own brands or cuts. Warnings seldom discourage a person intent on self-scarification, especially by cutting. In the view of Professor Myrna Armstrong of Texas Tech Medical Sciences Center, cutting patterns in the skin to create a scar "borders on self-mutilation."[12] In other words, people want to hurt themselves because it is their way of releasing psychological or emotional pain.

Indeed it is sometimes difficult to determine whether people who cut themselves are doing so because they want to create scar designs or because they are addicted to self-injury, or self-inflicted violence (SIV), a serious psychological problem. An estimated two to three million Americans engage in SIV. They carry psychological scars sometimes because they have been physically or sexually abused. Cutting, they say, relieves or dulls emotional pain, distress, frustration, or other negative feelings. After a cutting they frequently express a great sense of relief seeing the blood running down an arm, leg, or other part of the body. People who need help with self-injury problems can find information and advice on various Web sites. One of the sites that contains links to numerous resources is www.smalltime.com/notvictims/cutting.html.

Yet that does not mean all people who cut themselves to produce scars suffer a psychological disorder. In spite of the stigma attached to self-cuttings, numerous people who mark themselves in this manner are proud of their scarifications. Some contend that the process brings a level of awareness beyond anything imaginable. In this manner, they celebrate their bodies; their scars, they say, are unique artistic expressions displayed on their own skin.[13]

Strict safety precautions are required so that disease and infections are avoided.

Safe?

uestions about the safety of body art bring both negative and positive responses. Books and articles on the subject frequently address the pros and cons, as do numerous Web sites on tattooing, piercing, and scarification.

The naysayers are predominately health-care practitioners, from school nurses to doctors and dentists. The American Academy of Dermatology (AAD), for example, objects to all forms of body piercing except for the earlobe because of possible skin problems such as dermatitis, an inflammation of the skin, and infections.

The American Dental Association (ADA) condemns tongue, lip, or cheek piercing, calling the practice a public health hazard. Because the mouth hosts a lot of bacteria, the tongue can easily become infected after a piercing. Tongue piercings also can cause gum damage and chipped teeth. The jewelry inserted can affect one's speaking ability, perhaps causing a lisp, and chewing and swallowing may become difficult.[1]

According to The Nemours Foundation, a nonprofit organization that maintains a Web site called KidsHealth, "both the U.S. and Canadian Red Cross won't accept blood donations from anyone who has had a body piercing or tattoo within a year because both procedures can transmit dangerous blood-borne diseases."[2]

On the other side of the argument are those who contend that owners of reputable tattooing and body piercing studios or shops maintain a sanitary environment similar to that of a medical office. In the first place, they require any under-age person to have written parental consent that must be notarized and proper picture identification, such as a driver's license, for any type of body art or modification.

Reputable practitioners or artists are diligent about cleanliness. They use autoclave machines, and disinfect work area surfaces (tables and counters and the like). They make sure that needles, inkwells, razors, ointments, or other materials are discarded after a single use, including the latex gloves worn when they pierce or tattoo.

Safety Precautions

At a reputable tattoo shop, an artist first reviews the design that the customer has selected and asks that person to sign a release form. The form includes questions about age and blood-borne diseases, such as hepatitis or the human immunodeficiency virus (HIV) that causes AIDS.

The tattoo artist cleans, disinfects, and shaves the area to be tattooed, then lubricates it with a bit of petroleum jelly. The artist uses a stencil or gelatin-type duplicating paper to transfer an outline of the design onto the skin.

Tattoo artists usually use an electric handheld tattoo machine controlled with a foot pedal. Needles soldered onto a metal bar hold ink. The number of needles varies from one for fine-line tattooing to more than fifteen for tribal designs with large areas of black ink. Reputable artists use new needles for each client. The needles are sterilized and wrapped in paper. Many artists will open the needles in front of a client and examine the points with a magnifying glass to make sure they are sharp. They then pour the inks into tiny caps so that they do not risk contaminating the stock of ink. They also wear latex gloves to protect both the customer and themselves.

When the tattoo is finished, artists will most likely apply a thin coating of antibiotic ointment and provide the customer with oral and written instructions on taking care of the tattoo. Tattoo artists may also take a photograph of the tattoo for their portfolio.

A tattoo artist should be a member of a professional group such as the Alliance of Professional Tattooists (APT). Members must take a nine-hour safety seminar within two years of joining and must have operated for a minimum of three years in an established location. Because of the increasing popularity of body art and concerns about safety, lawmakers often talk of doing regular

A freestyle swimmer from Belgium gets a simple tattoo of the Olympic rings.

inspections at body art shops. The APT attempts to "promote the understanding that professional tattooing is a safe expression of art" and tries "to educate lawmakers, dispel myths and counter misinformation with researched fact," according to its Web site.[3]

Artists may also belong to the Association of Professional Piercers (APP). Part of APP's philosophy is the belief that "piercers must act ethically, responsibly, and be accountable for quality service." The association certifies piercers who agree to follow strict health and safety guidelines.

Nevertheless, even when performed under the most sanitary conditions, tattooing, piercing, branding, and cutting for scarification can pose health risks. The risks increase when body marking is done by amateurs or by so-called professionals in such places as flea markets, carnivals, and even in vans. People, especially adolescents, who tattoo, pierce, brand, or cut themselves or their friends are at most risk for health problems.

Another risky situation is the tattoo party. At this trendy event, friends get together to be tattooed by a practitioner hired for the occasion. In one reported instance, a mother hired a tattooist to come to her home to tattoo her daughter and her friends; the mother was concerned that a tattoo shop would not be safe. Yet sanitation in a reputable tattoo studio is likely to be better than it is in the average home. An artist usually gives his or her undivided attention to the tattoo, which is impossible when a group of friends are clustered around to watch. The standard tattoo shop requires visitors to stay behind a barrier to prevent distraction and contamination.

Health Hazards from Tattooing and Piercing

Skin is the body's protective barrier. Anytime the skin is punctured, cut, or burned, a person may be exposed to infection or a systemic illness, including HIV. For example, body piercing has been associated with the risk of HIV. As the U.S. Centers for Disease Control and Prevention (CDC) noted:

> Healing of piercings generally will take weeks, and sometimes even months, and the pierced tissue could conceivably be abraded (torn or cut) or inflamed even after healing. Therefore, a theoretical HIV transmission risk does exist if the unhealed or abraded tissues come into contact with an infected person's blood or other infectious body fluid. Additionally, HIV could be transmitted if instruments contaminated with blood are not sterilized or disinfected between clients.[4]

However, between 1985 and 1997, the CDC recorded no known cases of HIV transmission from tattooing and piercing. In 1999 the CDC again reported "no instances of HIV transmission" from these practices. But the CDC did note that an infectious disease called viral hepatitis can be spread by body piercing and tattooing if unsterilized equipment or needles are used.

Hepatitis is inflammation of the liver, the organ that helps process nutrients and medications and removes toxic wastes from the body. Proper liver functioning is vital for good health, and a severely damaged liver is life-threatening. Although there are six types of viral hepatitis (called A, B, C, D, E, and

G), the viruses B and C are the most serious, leading to cirrhosis and cancer of the liver. A vaccine is available to protect against hepatitis A and B, but no vaccine exists yet to prevent hepatitis C. According to the well-known Mayo Clinic in Rochester, Minnesota:

> The hepatitis B virus is spread through infected blood, blood products and body fluids. In addition to blood, hepatitis B virus can be found in semen, vaginal fluids and saliva. It is not found in urine or feces. Hepatitis B is frequently spread through sharing needles, sexual contact and from mother to baby at birth. It can also be spread by ear piercing, tattooing and acupuncture if equipment or needles are not sterilized between use.[5]

Hepatitis C may also be a consequence of tattooing and piercing. According to a 2001 report in *The New York Times*, Dr. Robert Haley of the University of Texas Southwestern Medical Center and Dr. Paul Fischer of the Presbyterian Hospital of Dallas studied 626 patients and "found that those with tattoos were nine times as likely to be infected with hepatitis C as people who were not." The study, published in March 2001 in the journal *Medicine*, was conducted at an orthopedic spinal clinic because patients were not there due to blood-borne infections. The study concluded that "one-third of the 52 patients who had gotten their tattoos at commercial tattoo parlors were infected with hepatitis C, compared with 3.5 percent of the patients without tattoos," the *Times* reported.[6]

Another health risk associated with body piercing is endocarditis, a bacterial infection of the heart valve. In a 1999 study, the Mayo Clinic found that out of 445 patients with congenital heart disease (who are at increased risk of heart valve infection) "nearly one out of four" with body piercings suffered "from infection as a result of the piercing. Only 6 percent took antibiotics preventively to fend off an infection." According to the study, most doctors "believe preventive antibiotics should be used by patients with heart disease who have body piercing or tattooing."[7]

People who have no previous or chronic health problems also risk bacterial infection from body piercing, even when it is done by a reputable artist under hygienic conditions and aftercare directions are followed. Infection is often the result of improper hygiene and piercings in areas of the body with high bacteria content. For example, upper ear piercings may become infected from bacteria in the hair. Coauthor Christine Whittington says even after the piercing of her upper ear cartilage appeared to be healed it became infected from her headset earphones, which she used while she was running.

Because piercings take weeks or months to heal, the risk of infection is prolonged. The ears, eyebrows, nose, lips, and tongue heal the most quickly, usually from six to eight weeks, while it takes eight weeks to nine months or more for the navel and nipple to heal.

The Health Information Network of the National Education Association (NEA) published a column on body art health risks, which points out:

> Navel piercings have a 45 percent infection rate because hygiene is generally poor in that area. The friction of tight clothing like waistbands also creates a moist environment where bacteria thrive . . . . Adolescents must understand that if they do a body piercing, they need to maintain a continual regimen of post-piercing skin care.[8]

Another common problem related to piercings is an allergic reaction to the jewelry. Jewelry that is brass-plated or contains nickel should not be used because the wound may fester and itch. To avoid a reaction, body jewelry must be made of surgical-grade stainless steel, titanium, or 14- or 18-karat gold.

Aftercare

Taking care of a tattoo or piercing after it is completed is crucial to body art safety. Most body art practitioners provide their customers with information sheets on how to care for a new tattoo or piercing. For example, award-winning artist Mike Balestrieri in Florida provides a tattoo aftercare sheet that is similar to what many other artists hand out. It advises:

- [tattoos] should be washed twice a day for the next two days to remove any blood residue on the skin. Wash tattoo with antibacterial soap and your hand only. Apply A & D ointment during the day as needed to keep your tattoo moist for the next two weeks.
- Take cool showers for the first week, please.
- No water activities for three weeks and no direct sunlight on your tattoo for 30 days.

- Do not scratch or pick at your tattoo.
- Remember to use sun block on your tattoo after it has healed to keep it looking new.[9]

Balestrieri, like other artists, provides even more detailed aftercare instructions for ear, facial, tongue, navel, and nipple piercing, warning in particular about keeping clean and not touching the pierced area. But some clients do not follow directions. For example, one teenage girl developed an infection after a tongue piercing. "She came back with her angry father, who was ready to jump all over me," Balestrieri said. "I explained to the father that the girl had been in earlier because she was concerned about an infection. She came with friends who told me she had been to a party right after her piercing and was kissing guys on the neck! All that sweat and skin contact can easily cause a bacterial infection."[10] In short, the girl ignored the cardinal rule following a piercing: Do not touch the pierced area except for daily cleanings.

Information about aftercare is also available on numerous Web sites, including an online continuing education course for nurses. Along with other healthcare professionals, nurses today are frequently seeing patients with some type of body adornment. Among the varied instructions that appear on the nurses' Web site, as well as in aftercare instructions provided by artists, is the advice on how to reduce swelling after tongue piercing. Sucking on ice cubes and rinsing with salt water are recommended. The cleansing method suggested for lip and navel piercing is soap and water.[11]

If there is a problem with healing or an infection, a medical doctor or nurse practitioner may have to be consulted. A prescription medication might be needed to deal with the infection. Perhaps a person suffers a pull-through injury when piercing jewelry catches on clothing, a blanket, or other object, then pulls out of the hole and tears the skin. Such an injury could require plastic surgery.

Removing or Altering Body Art..........

Most types of body art are designed to be permanent, except for a piercing, which closes up when the jewelry is removed. But countless individuals decide years after being tattooed or branded that their body art should go or at least be changed. Altering a brand or tattoo design is usually less expensive than removal.

This series of images shows the progression and final result of a successful tattoo cover-up.

There are numerous reasons that people want to remove tattoos. One of the foremost is a change in relationships. After a bitter divorce, for example, a person is likely to want her or his spouse's name or picture "erased." One man in Florida had a picture of his wife tattooed on his chest, but after a divorce asked a tattoo artist to turn her into an elderly man complete with wrinkled skin. Another divorcé said he "buried" his former wife under a mountain on his bicep, "the tattoo artist created a mountain scene that completely covered my ex-wife's name."[12]

Some people have body art removed or changed because it was done by an amateur and the design is fuzzy, a mere blob of ink, or an unidentifiable scar. Body art may also be unacceptable in the workplace. In some cases, body markings—particularly tattoos—show a previous affiliation with a gang or prison life, which the person may want to renounce.

To deal with gang tattoo removal, numerous volunteer programs have been set up across the United States. Most of these programs maintain Web sites, which can be found with a simple search for "tattoo removal programs." Sister June Wilkerson at the Providence Holy Cross Medical Center in Mission Hills, California, opened a clinic in 1998 to serve former gang members, prostitutes, ex-convicts, white supremacists, and others who want to change their images by surgically removing their tattoos. Those who are accepted for tattoo removal are required to perform community service.[13]

The Salt Lake City police department in conjunction with the University of Utah set up a tattoo removal program in 1991 for former gang members only. The University's Medical Center provides, free-of-charge, the physicians and other health-care professionals and the equipment necessary for this service. To be eligible, individuals cannot have an arrest record for one year prior to applying for tattoo removal and they "must be involved in activities which will prevent their future involvement in gang activity (i.e., school, employment, counseling)."[14]

Although tattoo removal services are available free for former gang members and ex-convicts, others who want to rid themselves of their body marks must pay the cost, which ranges from several hundred dollars to thousands of dollars. To remove some large tattoos, several visits to the doctor may be required. Medical insurance seldom covers such services because the procedures are considered cosmetic rather than medically necessary.

How is a tattoo removed? Usually by a specialist in dermatology who is qualified to use laser technology (the word laser is an acronym for *light amplification by stimulated emission of radiation*). Some doctors may use older methods, such as freezing the skin before removing the tattoo or "sanding" the skin in a process called dermabrasion. In some cases, a surgeon may have to cut the skin to remove a large tattoo or brand and sew up the wound. Grafting skin, cutting it from another part of the body to replace the tattooed or branded skin, may also be necessary. But for the most part today, laser surgery is the method of choice for tattoo removal.

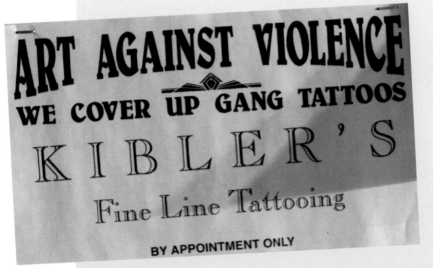

David "Kibler" Scott, the owner of this establishment in Illinois, specializes in covering up or removing gang-related tattoos.

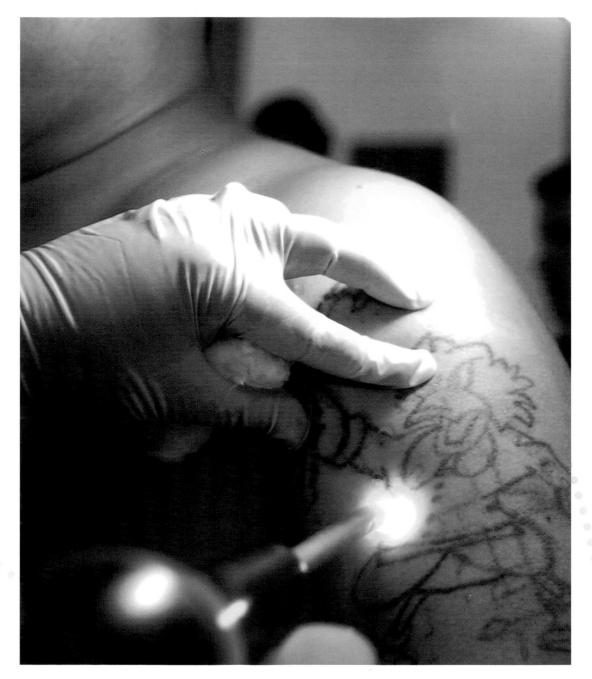

A young man receives laser treatment to remove a tattoo as part of the "Goodbye to Tattoos" program organized by the Catholic Church of Honduras. In Honduras, tattoos are considered symbols of crime. More than six thousand people have returned to society after participating in this program.

Laser beams penetrate the skin and attack the tattoo ink, breaking it into tiny bits that are consumed by the body's scavenger cells. Various lasers for tattoo removal use different high-energy pulses (light flashes) in a technique called q-switching: q-switched ruby, q-switched alexandrite, and q-switched Nd:YAG. Each laser attacks different colors. Black ink is the easiest to remove because the color absorbs all wavelengths of laser light, while green and yellow are the most difficult to break down.

Does it hurt? In a word, Yes. Some describe the procedure as merely uncomfortable, while others say the laser pulses are like getting zapped with a rubber band or splatters of hot grease. Nevertheless, most people will accept the pain as well as the price if they want to be free of body marks.

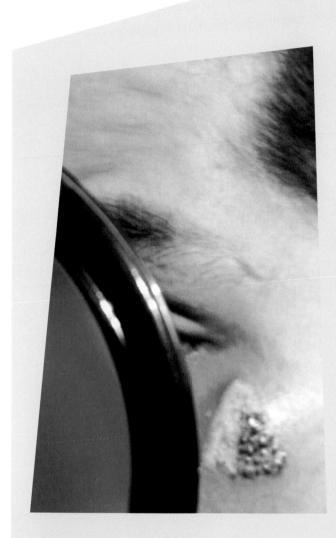

The results of the first step in removing a gang tattoo

Tattoo and Piercing

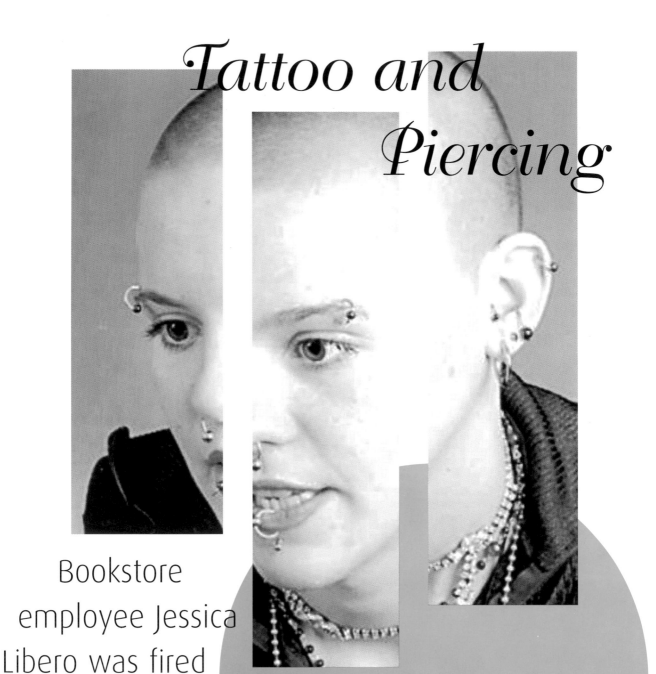

Bookstore employee Jessica Libero was fired from Atticus Bookstore Café in New Haven, Connecticut, because she would not remove her facial rings and studs.

Taboos and Laws

Even though body marks and modifications are much more acceptable in the United States today than they were twenty to thirty years ago, taboos still exist. It's not likely that a person with multiple ear piercings or numerous tattoos on the arms will be allowed to work as a bank teller, school nurse, or waiter in a fine-dining establishment. Such workers, along with many others in the public eye, usually have to abide by employer rules (written or unwritten) regarding appearance in the workplace. Certainly the military regulates what servicemen and -women can or cannot wear on their bodies.

Town and city officials also regulate (or attempt to control) body art. Some may oppose body art, believing that tattoo studios are "dens of iniquity," as they were so often labeled in the past. They believe that such businesses harm the community, and they try to ban them. Other officials are more concerned about safety issues and pass ordinances or laws to protect public health.

Taboos in the Workplace

"Hey, I ought to be judged on how I work, not on whether I have tattoos or piercings!" That's the opinion of many young people in the workplace. Most employers, however, have a different view. They believe that body piercing, tattoos, neon hair-coloring, and similar fashions are extreme and

could bring negative reactions from customers, scaring them away. Most businesses want their employees to present professional images, so they do not allow them to have any type of piercings, except for the traditional fashion of pierced earrings on women, and all tattoos have to be covered. According to a Knight-Ridder business news report from Indianapolis, Indiana, "Blockbuster Video restricts front-line employees to one earring per ear and prohibits any other visible piercing. Taco Bell has a similar policy. At the Indianapolis-based Steak n Shake restaurant chain, employees are not allowed to don any visible tattoos or body art while on the job."[1]

Vince Cancasci, the young California man with his fifteen tats, keeps his body art covered while at work. As he notes, "I sure wouldn't have the job I have now if I had tattoos where I really wanted them. I would be deemed unfit to perform my duties, because a part of my skin would scare people." In his view, this constitutes "the most blatant act of discrimination employers use on a daily basis."[2]

Even older workers must abide by body art rules at some places of business. In Illinois, a retired educator and ex-serviceman took a part-time job at Six Flags Great America, where, he said, "I had to cover up my faded tattoo from World War II days." But he soon quit the job because he was required to wear a long-sleeved shirt under the short-sleeved uniform shirt in the sweltering summer weather. "I could understand the rule," he said, "but I simply was not willing to be that uncomfortable for minimum wage!"[3]

In a similar situation, Michael Riggs, a policeman with the Fort Worth, Texas, Police Department, had acquired colorful tattoos on his arms and legs when he was in the U.S. Army. But after several years on the police force, Riggs was not allowed to wear his summer uniform consisting of a short-sleeved shirt and short pants, which revealed his "extensive tattoos." The police chief said that Riggs's tattoos detracted from "the professionalism of a Fort Worth police officer," even though the department has no policy regarding tattoos. Riggs was required to wear a long-sleeved shirt and long pants. According to a news story, "Officer Riggs was hospitalized for two days [in July 2001] with symptoms of heat exhaustion, which doctors said were brought on by wearing long sleeves in the heat." Claiming unfair treatment, the officer filed a civil rights lawsuit.[4]

Other employers are more lenient, depending on the kind of business operation. Music stores and some theaters that cater to young customers, for example, may allow their employees to wear multiple earrings and other piercings as well as to display their tattoos. Geographical location is a factor also. Workers with body art are more widely accepted on the East and West coasts, where trends and fads are often initiated, than they are in the more conservative Midwest. Also, businesses in college and university towns are more likely to allow their employees to display their body art than would businesses in other communities.

Religious Taboos

Throughout history, some religious groups have forbidden body markings or modifications. A basic principle of Jewish teaching is that "no one has complete ownership of his or her own body. God gives a person his or her body for safekeeping. Therefore self-mutilation or any form of attack upon the body is viewed as a breach of this trust," writes Joel Grishaver, who teaches classes on Jewish law and ethics and is a renowned Jewish writer.[5] According to Jewish religious law in the Torah, Leviticus 19:28 states: "You shall not cut into your flesh—for soul driven reasons—nor shall you write a tattoo on yourselves—I am Adonai [the Lord]." Those who cut themselves for "soul driven reasons" followed a custom of ancient Amorite people who cut their flesh when someone among them died. In order to distinguish themselves from this other local culture, Jews denounced and repudiated the Amorites' cutting practices.

Permanent body marks not only are seen as mutilation of the body in Jewish teaching, but also were once used to identify slaves and were "pagan practices"—customs followed by those who worshiped idols. The Nazi practice of tattooing Jewish prisoners during World War II was especially repugnant because it was a clear sign that Jews were being branded like cattle for the Holocaust slaughter.

In biblical times, piercings also indicated lifelong slavery, and the cartilage of the ear, not the flesh, was pierced so that the opening would never close. Yet not all flesh or even cartilage piercings are prohibited in Judaism. Some body piercings are allowed or acceptable if they do not leave permanent marks (or holes); are safe and modest; are used to beautify or decorate, not to bring pain; and if they are not connected with pagan practices, which today usually means non-Jewish customs.[6]

It is a common belief that Jewish law prohibits burial in a Jewish cemetery if a person has a tattoo. However, numerous rabbis have pointed out

that even if a person violates a Jewish law, such as eating shellfish or lighting a fire on the Sabbath, that does not ban him or her from burial in a Jewish cemetery. Rabbi Barry H. Block explained:

> The rights and privileges of being a Jew—the honor of reading from the Torah, of kindling Sabbath light, and even of burial in the cemetery—are frequently accorded to Jews who ignore one Jewish law or another. A person who has a tattoo should be treated as no less worthy than one who doesn't always observe the Sabbath or fast on Yom Kippur. Though we take all of these requirements seriously, we do not turn away Jews who do not follow every one. We certainly do not reject a young Jew whose most serious crime is a silly tattoo.[7]

Christians as well as Jews have forbidden or denounced tattooing, also citing Leviticus 19:28, but in a different manner: "Ye shall not make any cuttings on your flesh for the dead nor print any marks upon you." However, tattooing was practiced among early Christians, and the bans were more likely against tattoos that adorned those considered "heathens." Tattooing was banned under Pope Hadrian in A.D. 786, but this brought great dissent. The prohibition was rescinded less than twenty years later.

Military Regulations

While it has been a long tradition for sailors, soldiers, and others in the armed services to get tattooed, the U.S. military has never tolerated body adornments that detract from the uniform. But the increasing popularity of tattooing, piercing, and branding during the 1990s prompted some branches of the U.S. military to establish detailed regulations regarding body art. U.S. Army regulations on "Wear and Appearance of Army Uniforms and Insignia"(AR 670-1) were changed in 1998 to prohibit tattoos or brands that:

(1) show an alliance with "extremist" organizations.
(2) are indecent (i.e., those which are grossly offensive to modesty, decency, or propriety; shock the moral sense because of their vulgar, filthy, or disgusting nature; tend to incite lustful thought; or tend reasonably to corrupt morals or incite libidinous thoughts).[8]

Unreasonably large or excessively numerous tattoos (for example, a series of tattoos covering the majority of one or more limbs) are also prohibited. Tattoos or brands visible on the head, face, or neck are banned as well. Usually small, inconspicuous tattoos or brands are allowed, but when a soldier wears a Class A uniform, which equates with civilian business attire, a tattoo or brand must not detract from a soldierly appearance, that is, make the soldier appear unprofessional or undisciplined.[9]

What if a tattoo or brand violates regulations? A commander first advises a soldier about noncompliance with AR 670-1 and available medical tattoo removal services. Soldiers can have their tattoos removed at a number of locations, such as an Army Community Hospital or Troop Medical Clinic. In mid-2000, the Walter Reed Army Medical Center in Washington, D.C., inaugurated a new laser center for active-duty service personnel. Doctors at the center treat people from the Army, Air Force, Navy, and Marine Corps, removing tattoos free for active duty personnel and charging relatively low fees for dependents.[10]

The Army policy regarding piercings prohibits "attaching, affixing, or displaying objects, articles, jewelry or ornamentation to or through the skin while in uniform, in civilian clothes, while on duty, or in civilian clothes off duty on any military installation or other places under Army control."[11] Although male soldiers are not authorized to wear any type of earring when in uniform or when wearing civilian clothing on duty, earrings on female soldiers are an exception. Women are authorized to wear earrings on Army installations while on duty in civilian attire and may also wear approved earrings while in uniform.[12]

Other branches of the military have issued similar regulations. Major James McGarrahan, United States Marine Corp (USMC), noted: "As a Marine commander, my rule of thumb in practice follows generally accepted USMC traditions and practices, that is, that tattoos are permitted, albeit with some restrictions." Major McGarrahan said those restrictions, which are similar to those outlined for the Army, include location on the body, content, and size. In the major's words:

> Tattoos are not permitted above the collar line (head, face, neck, ears) for any personnel; for officers, the general rule is they should not be visible in a short-sleeved shirt, but Mustangs (those who rise from the ranks to become officers)

are allowed some grace for the time they spent as an enlisted Marine. Anything visible must be in generally good taste using the "reasonable man" standard; tattoos containing obscene, sexually explicit, racist, or other text or graphic content which would bring discredit upon the Corps are forbidden; violent images, such as blood, guts, combat stuff, are not encouraged, but not prohibited, and many Marines have them. In general, a few reasonably sized images are accepted, but making a major section of the body into a billboard is not acceptable.

Piercing and branding, of any kind, in any place on the body, for any reason, are not permitted, and are normally "discouraged" through the military justice system (either non-judicial punishment or court-martial depending on the specifics of the case). The exception are pierced ears for women Marines—even these must be low-profile, discreet, and worn in a manner not intended to attract a lot of attention. Male Marines are prohibited from piercing their ears or wearing head-jewelry at any time.[13]

Regulations also apply at military schools. At the Naval Academy, for example, "Tattoos, brands and body piercing (other than a single perforation of each earlobe) are discouraged. No tattoo or brand may be visible when wearing regulation PE gear (gym clothes: in general, shirt sleeves covering half the upper arm and shorts covering half the thigh). All tattoos or brands which are prejudicial to good order and discipline, offensive, or are of such a nature as to bring discredit upon the naval service are prohibited."[14]

Similar rules apply at the U.S. Air Force Academy. In its catalog, the Academy tells applicants that those who review them as candidates for admission "are of an older generation" and may not view tattoos, brands, or piercings in the same manner as an applicant does. The Academy offers the kind of advice given in many other segments of society: "If you don't already have a tattoo or brand, think long and hard as to whether the risk of possibly losing out on an Academy appointment [or job, or promotion] is worth it."[15]

..... What's the Law?

Although tattooing has been outlawed in some states, it is now legal in most. However, state and local laws restrict body art practices. These laws are not uniform across the United States, but most states require a person under the

age of eighteen to have parental or guardian consent for a tattoo or piercing. The state penal code in California forbids any person to tattoo or offer to tattoo someone under the age of eighteen. Doing so is a misdemeanor. The code also states: "It shall be an infraction for any person to perform or offer to perform body piercing upon a person under the age of 18 years, unless the body piercing is performed in the presence of, or as directed by a notarized writing by, the person's parent or guardian."[16]

Massachusetts banned all tattooing in the 1960s due to a hepatitis scare, but in late 2000 the ban was overturned. Massachusetts Superior Court Judge Barbara Rouse found the law unconstitutional—a violation of free speech. She noted in her decision, that the ban "promoted an underground tattoo industry with no controls."[17] Now cities and towns in the state have jurisdiction over tattoo studios. One example is New Bedford, whose health department enforces regulations that prohibit anyone under the influence of alcohol or other drugs from getting a tattoo. Also prohibited are tattooing of the genitalia and scarification practices. In addition, mobile tattoo parlors are outlawed.

Anyone who wants to open a tattoo studio in New Bedford must "submit an application that includes a detailed floor plan of their establishment, to ensure that the tattoo parlor meets a long list of criteria aimed at protecting the public's health." According to a news report: "A tattoo practitioner must have documentation that he or she has completed courses on blood-borne pathogens, first aid, anatomy, and skin diseases. Licenses from other states will be considered as proof of experience."[18]

Most reputable artists in Massachusetts and other states agree that there should be some regulation of their industry, particularly in regard to public health and safety. As in Massachusetts, a health department is usually responsible for licensing and regulating tattoo artists. In most states a tattoo artist must have a qualified license to practice, which is issued only if the applicant passes an examination and pays the appropriate fee. A license may be revoked for a variety of reasons, including incompetence, negligence, and addiction to alcohol or other substances.

The Body as

On September 21, 2001, people of all ages lined up at a tattoo shop in Los Angeles to receive a variety of patriotic tattoos in response to the terrorist attacks of September 11.

a Canvas or a Billboard?

On any given day, someone decides to take the plunge and use her or his body as a canvas for tattoo art or to record life experiences. As one writer explained:

> Of all the raw materials available to humanity for transformation into art, the body is the most readily available. The marking of the body is often a human being's first expression of individuality, the putting of something of the inner self on the outer skin. The body art of tattooing is a personal means of immediate self-expression, a permanent visible statement of self.[1]

There is little doubt that most people who decorate or modify their bodies strongly believe they are expressing their individuality. Their body art is akin to a universal language that has no social and economic barriers. They believe that others who have "been there" can relate to the process of marking the skin as well as to the variety of messages being conveyed with body art.

Yet so many people have body marks today that some observers wonder whether tattooing, piercing, and scarification are part of a trend or a fad rather than being forms of creative expression. Are people wearing body marks in order to be accepted into a particular group rather than displaying their individuality? Do body marks signal that peer pressure has won out over independence?

Then there are some people who appear to be walking billboards with their body marks. What, for example, does a tattoo representing a motion picture, a rock band, or sports team really say? Is a person's skin being used as an advertising backdrop?

Since there is no field guide for determining what tattoos signify, their meaning is understood only by the person with the tattoo and those who know the story behind it. Consider the meaning of a number 13, for example. The only certainty is that the person with that tattoo chose to be marked with the image at some point in his or her life.

Some questions are more practical in nature, particularly when it comes to laws, dress codes, health concerns, and social and religious taboos associated with body marks. On the following pages are some Frequently Asked Questions.

This "Made In The U.S.A." tattoo was placed on September 20, 2001, above a five-year-old eye-for-an-eye tattoo to convey a very intentional message by the wearer.

FAQs

Q. Why have states passed Parental Consent laws to get a tattoo or piercing?
A. The laws are designed to protect minors who may not understand the health risks associated with unsanitary tattoo and piercing studios.

Q. Do some schools have dress codes that forbid tattooing or body piercing?
A. Yes. Some religious schools require modest dress and adornment. One example is the Church of Jesus Christ and Latter-day Saints' Brigham Young University. The university's dress code states that earrings and body piercings are not acceptable for men and that "excessive ear piercing" (meaning more than one hole per ear) and body piercing are not acceptable for women.

Q. Will a tattoo become infected if an amateur does it?
A. Chances are much greater that an amateur's tattoo equipment is not as sanitary as that used in a legitimate and reputable tattoo studio.

Q. Aren't most piercings done by licensed people?
A. No. There are no federal regulations governing body piercing, and only recently have states begun to pass laws requiring businesses to follow health and safety standards for piercing. Piercers in jewelry stores, hair salons, and similar businesses are seldom licensed to practice body piercing.

Q. After a piercing heals, why is it necessary to continue daily cleansing?
A. Cleaning once a day keeps dead skin cells and dirt from accumulating at the piercing site.

Q. Some people believe they should be able to display tattoos and wear piercing jewelry when they go for a job interview. Will that diminish their chances of getting the job?

A. In many cases, yes. Conservative dress and appearance are still more acceptable for a job interview.

Q. What can people do if they have tattoos that look like, but are not, gang symbols?

A. The tattoos can be surgically removed (an expensive process) or covered up by a tattoo artist who incorporates the original symbol within a new design.

Q. Can every tattoo be completely removed?

A. *Complete* tattoo removal may not be possible, dermatologists say.

Q. Are there any side effects when a tattoo is surgically removed?

A. Sometimes after a tattoo is removed the skin becomes darker in color at the removal site (hyperpigmentation) or the skin loses its normal color (hypopigmentation). Other rare side effects include infection or scarring at the site.

Q. Why is it illegal in some states to tattoo above the collar or on the hands and feet?

A. The reasons are not specified, but regulations may be based on the military model that bans such visible tattoos or they could be based on the fact that the healing process is more difficult at these sites.

Q. Is it OK to copy someone's custom tattoo design?

A. Copying someone's custom design is considered unethical in the body art world. Some tattoo artists won't even duplicate a mummy's tattoos, because they say the tattoo belongs to the person who wore it. But an exception to the taboo is children and grandchildren reproducing tattoos of parents or grandparents so that the tattoo will "live on."

Q. Do colors in a tattoo fade?
A. Sometimes. To prevent fading, artists recommend a strong sun-block for people who spend a lot of time in the sun.

Q. What areas of the body are most painful when getting a tattoo?
A. Pain depends on the individual, but generally tattooing areas over the bone such as the ankle, collarbone, chest, ribs, and spine can be painful for many individuals.

Q. Is it possible to have a piercing or tattoo done with a local anesthetic?
A. Some piercers and tattoo artists do offer local anesthetics (sometimes for an extra charge), but most do not. The discomfort in both cases is usually tolerable and is part of the experience, especially when endorphins (natural pain relievers) begin to work.

Q. What happens if a person drinks alcohol or takes drugs before getting a tattoo?
A. Reputable artists don't allow any drug use, including drinking alcohol, in their establishments. Alcohol can thin the blood, causing a person to bleed easily, and a person using drugs may become unruly.

Q. If a woman has a tattoo on the abdomen or a navel ring, what happens when she gets pregnant?
A. A tattoo on the abdomen stretches during pregnancy, and after the baby is born the tattoo might not appear as it did originally. The navel changes shape during pregnancy, and piercing jewelry could become uncomfortable if not impossible to wear. To diminish health risks, many women remove piercing jewelry during pregnancy.

Q. Are tattoo designs from flash found on lots of people?
A. Yes. Choosing a tattoo from flash is similar to buying clothing "off the rack." However, a good tattoo artist can alter the design in some way to make it more personal.

Q. Will body art and modification still be popular in the years ahead?
A. If history is any indication, no doubt some form of marking and modifying the body will endure in the future. Also, as body art continues to move into the mainstream, some of its collectors and practitioners will challenge themselves with more intricate and difficult styles of tattooing, piercing, and scarring. Others, wishing to move beyond the mainstream, will look for new and more "extreme" ways to modify their bodies.

For Further Information

Articles

Bronnikov, Arkady G. "Telltale Tattoos in Russian Prisons." *Natural History* 102, no. 11 (November 1993), 50–60.

Burg, B. R. "Tattoo Designs and Locations in the Old U.S. Navy." *Journal of American Culture* 18, no. 1 (Spring 1995), 69–76.

DeMello, Margo. "'Not Just for Bikers Anymore': Popular Representations of American Tattooing." *Journal of Popular Culture* 29, no. 2 (Fall 1995), 37–53.

Mayor, Adrienne. "People Illustrated." *Archaeology* 52, no. 2 (March/April 1999), 4–7.

Newman, Simon P. "Reading the Bodies of Early American Seafarers." *William & Mary Quarterly* 55, no. 1 (January 1998), 59–83.

Polosmak, Natalya, and Charles O'Rear. "A Mummy Unearthed from the Pastures of Heaven." *National Geographic* 186, no. 4 (October 1994), 80–102.

Books

Beckwith, Carol, and Angela Fisher. *African Ceremonies*. 2 vols. New York: Abrams, 1999.

Brain, Robert. *The Decorated Body*. New York: Harper & Row, 1979.

Burchett, George. *Memoirs of a Tattooist: From the Notes, Diaries, and Letters of the Late "King of Tattooists," George Burchett*. London: Oldbourne, 1958.

Caplan, Jane, ed. *Written on the Body: The Tattoo in European and American History*. Princeton, NJ: Princeton University Press, 2000.

Collins, Sailor Jerry. *Sailor Jerry Collins, American Tattoo Master: In His Own Words*. Honolulu: Hardy Marks, 1994.

Graves, Bonnie B. *Tattooing and Body Piercing (Perspectives on Physical Health/LifeMatters Books)*. Mankato, MN: Capstone Press, 2000.

Hambly, Wilfrid. *The History of Tattooing and Its Significance: With Some Account of Other Forms of Corporal Marking*. London: H. F. & G. Witherby, 1925.

Hewitt, Kim. *Mutilating the Body: Identity in Blood and Ink*. Bowling Green, OH: Bowling Green State University Popular Press, 1997.

Lucas, Don, and Paula Lucas. *A narrative biography of Franklin Paul Rogers . . . the father of American tattooing; from the notes, photo albums, and interviews of the late F. Paul Rogers*. New Orleans: Lucas Enterprises, 1990.

Mannix, Daniel P. *Memoirs of a Sword Swallower*. San Francisco: V/Search, 1996.

McCabe, Michael. *New York City Tattoo: The Oral History of an Urban Art*. Honolulu: Hardy Marks, 1997.

Parry, Albert. *Tattoo; secrets of a strange art as practised among the natives of the United States*. New York: Simon and Schuster, 1933.

Reybold, Laura. *Everything You Need to Know About the Dangers of Tattooing and Body Piercing*. New York: Rosen, 1995.

Rudenko, S. I. *Frozen Tombs of Siberia: The Pazyryk Burials of Iron Age Horsemen*. Berkeley: University of California Press, 1970.

Sanders, Clinton. *Customizing the Body: The Art and Culture of Tattooing*. Philadelphia: Temple University Press, 1989.

Sinclair, Leonard L. "Stoney," and Alan B. Govenar. *Stoney Knows How: Life as a Tattoo Artist: Tattooing Since 1928*. Lexington, KY: University Press of Kentucky, 1981.

Spindler, Konrad. *The Man in the Ice: The Discovery of a 5,000-Year-Old Body Reveals the Secrets of the Stone Age*. New York: Harmony Books, 1994.

Wilkinson, Beth. *Coping with the Dangers of Tattooing, Body Piercing, and Branding*. New York: Rosen, 1998.

Winkler, Kathleen. *Tattooing and Body Piercing: Understanding the Risks*. Berkeley Heights, NJ: Enslow, 2002.

Web Sites

American Museum of Natural History, "Body Art: Marks of Identity," http://www.amnh.org/exhibitions/bodyart

Australian Museum Online, "Body Art," http://www.austmus.gov.au/bodyart/

Discovery.com, "The Human Canvas," http://www.discovery.com/exp/humancanvas/human-canvas.html

The Mariners' Museum, "Skin Deep: The Art of the Tattoo," http://www.mariner.org/exhibits/tattoo/index.htm

University of Pennsylvania Museum of Archaeology and Anthropology, "Bodies of Cultures," http://www.upenn.edu/museum/Exhibits/bodmodintro.html

Source Notes

Chapter 1

1. Steve Holden, "Tattoos and Piercings: Are They You?" *Tartan Online* (April 4, 2001, http://www.thetartan.com/vnews/display.v/ART/2001/04/04/3aca8393e9872?in_archive=1).
2. Alisha Woolerly, "Art for the Body," *The Enquirer and The Post, Cincinnati.Com* (March 28, 2001, http://cincinnati.com/freetime/032801_tattoos.html).
3. Sonya Padgett, "Tattoos: Under Their Skin," *Las Vegas Review-Journal* (November 14, 2000, http://www.lvrj.com/lvrj_home/2000/Nov-14-Tue-2000/living/14787313.html).
4. Vince Cancasci, correspondence with author Kathlyn Gay (May 2001).
5. Maureen Mercury, Photographs by Steve Haworth, *Pagan Fleshworks: The Alchemy of Body Modification* (Rochester, VT: Park Street Press, 2000), p. 5.
6. Kevin Heinrichs, "Tattoos No Longer Taboo?" *Christianity Today* (May 24, 1999), pp. 6, 17.
7. American Museum of Natural History, "Exhibition Highlights," *Body Art: Marks of Identity* (November 20, 1999–May 29, 2000, http://www.amnh.org/exhibitions/bodyart/exhibition_highlights.html).

Chapter 2

1. Paul G. Bahn, *The Cambridge Illustrated History of Prehistoric Art* (Cambridge: Cambridge University Press, 1998), p. 81.
2. Bahn, p. 72.
3. Bahn, pp. 75–76.
4. Catherine Cartwright Jones, "Where Did Henna Come From?—A Short History of Henna," *The Henna Page* (http://www.hennapage.com/henna/faq/faq3.html).
5. "A Mehndi Tutorial" (http://www.geocities.com/mehndiart/four.html).

6. Rufus C. Camphausen, *Return of the Tribal: A Celebration of Body Ornament* (Rochester, VT: Park Street Press, 1997), p. 53.
7. Marthe Péquart and Saint-Juste Péquart, "Grotte du Mas d'Azil (Ariège), une nouvelle galerie magdalénienne," *Annales de Paléontologie* 48 (1962), pp. 211–214, cited in Steve Gilbert, *Tattoo History Source Book* (New York: Juno Books, 2000), p. 11.
8. Bahn, p. 75.
9. Ben Harder, "Murder Mystery on Ice," *U.S. News & World Report* (August 6, 2001), p. 43.
10. South Tyrol Museum of Archaeology (http://www.archaeologiemuseum.it/f06_ice_uk.html)
11. Konrad Spindler, *The Man in the Ice* (New York: Harmony, 1994), p. 169.
12. Leopold Dorfer et al., "A Medical Report from the Stone Age?" *Lancet* (September 18, 1999), p. 1023.
13. Dorfer.
14. M. Moser et al., "Are Ötzi's Tattoos Acupuncture?" *Archaeology* (January/February 1999), p. 17.
15. Luigi Capasso, "5300 Years Ago the Ice Man Used Natural Laxatives and Antibiotics," *Lancet* (December 5, 1998), p. 1864; Spindler, 116.
16. Robert S. Bianchi, "Tattoo in Ancient Egypt," *Marks of Civilization*, by Arnold Rubin (Los Angeles: Museum of Cultural History, University of California, 1988), p. 22.
17. Gilbert, p. 13; Bianchi, p. 23.
18. Bianchi, pp. 23–24.
19. S. I. Rudenko, *Frozen Tombs of Siberia* (Berkeley: University of California Press, 1970), pp. 110–114; Leopold Dorfer et al., "A Medical Report from the Stone Age?" *Lancet* (September 18, 1999), p. 1023.
20. Natalya Polosmak, "A Mummy Unearthed From the Pastures of Heaven," *National Geographic* (October 1994), pp. 80–103.
21. Bahn, pp. 79–80; Johnson, Clarke UIC Oral Sciences OSCI 590: Hominid Evolution, Dental Anthropology, and Human Variation (Web site for University of Illinois at Chicago College of Dentistry course]: Section 6.1: "The Cultural Modification of Teeth." (http://www.uic.edu/classes/osci/osci590/6_1TheCulturalModificationOfTeeth.htm); drilled and inlaid teeth were very common among the Maya (author Christine Whittington's husband, archaeologist Stephen Whittington, found filed and drilled teeth to accommodate inlays on Maya skeletons from burials in Copán, Honduras).
22. Bahn, p. 78.
23. University of Iowa Health Care Medical Museum, "The Shaped Skull," *The Cultural Body: Alterations* (http://www.uihealthcare.com/depts/medmuseum/ wallexhibits/body/alterations/shapedskull.html).
24. University of California San Francisco's Electronic Daily, "Foot-Binding Custom Has Caused Disabilities in Chinese Women" (November 4, 1997, http://www.ucsf.edu/ daybreak/1997/11/1104_foot.htm).
25. Discovery.com, "Myanma (Burma) and Thailand: Neck Rings," *The Human Canvas* (http://www.discovery.com/exp/humancanvas/atlasburma.html).

26. C. P. Jones, "Stigma and Tattoo," *Written on the Body: The Tattoo in European and American History* (ed. Jane Caplan, Princeton, N.J.: Princeton University Press, 2000), pp. 2–8.

27. Jones, pp. 11–12.

28. Jones, pp. 4–5.

29. Gilbert, p. 15.

30. Jones, pp. 1–8.

31. "The Mark of the Legion" in "The Roman Army," p. 14, *Illustrated History of the Roman Empire* (www.roman-empire.net/army/army.html).

32. American Institute of Archaeology, "Questions About Greece and Rome," *Ask Dr. Dig* (2001, http://dig.archaeology.org/drdig/greece/38.html).

33. Gilbert, p. 151.

34. John Carswell, *Coptic Tattoo Designs* (Beirut: The American University of Beirut).

35. Diego de Landa, *Yucatán Before and After the Conquest* (New York: Dover, 1978), p. 35.

36. Wes Christensen, "A Fashion for Ecstasy: Maya Body Modifications," *Modern Primitives: An Investigation of Contemporary Adornment and Ritual* (ed. V. Vale and A. Juno, San Francisco: Re/Search Publications, 1989), p. 84.

37. Bruce Grant, *Concise Encyclopedia of the American Indian* (New York: Bonanza Books, 1989), p. 305; Lars Krutak, "The Arctic," *Tattoos.com Ezine* (http://www.tattoos.com/ARCTIC.htm).

38. Bahn, p. 76.

39. Bahn, p. 81.

Chapter 3

1. Edward Tagart, *A Memoir of the Late Captain Peter Heywood, R.N.; with Extracts from his Diaries and Correspondence* (London: E. Wilson, 1832), p. 83.

2. National Maritime Museum, Captain Cook (http://www.nmm.ac.uk/education/fact_files/fact_cook.html).

3. Joseph Banks, *Endeavour Journal of Joseph Banks* (ed. J. C. Beaglehole, 2 vol., Sydney: Angus & Robertson), reprinted in Steve Gilbert, *Tattoo History: A Source Book* (San Francisco: Juno Books, 2000), pp. 36–37.

4. Banks.

5. Joseph Banks, *The Endeavour Journal of Joseph Banks*, (ed. J. C. Beaglehole, Sydney: Angus & Robertson), vol. 1, p. 400, cited by Gilbert, p. 35–36.

6. Sydney Parkinson, *Journal of a Voyage to the South Seas* (London: C. Dilly, 1784, reprint ed. London: Caliban Books, 1984).

7. Steve Gilbert, *Tattoo History: A Source Book* (San Francisco: Juno Books, 2000), pp. 36–37.

8.   Stephan Oettermann, "On Display: Tattooed Entertainers in American and Germany," *Written on the Body: the Tattoo in European and American History* (ed. Jane Caplan, Princeton, NJ: Princeton University Press, 2000), p. 196.

9.   William Bligh, *Awake Bold Bligh!: William Bligh's Letters Describing the Mutiny on HMS Bounty* (Honolulu: University of Hawaii Press, 1989), pp. 84–86.

10. George Burchett, *Memoirs of a Tattooist* (London: Oldbourne, 1958), pp. 100–101.

11. Burchett, pp. 207–211.

12. Oettermann, pp. 193–194.

13. Gilbert, pp. 126–127.

14. Gilbert, p. 129.

15. Oettermann, pp. 193–194.

16. Gilbert, p. 129.

17. Gilbert, p. 136.

18. Leonard Cassuto, "'What an Object He Would Have Made of Me!': Tattooing and the Racial Freak in Melville's *Typee*," in *Freakery: Cultural Spectacles of the Extraordinary Body* (ed. Rosemarie Garland Thomson, New York: New York University Press, 1996), p. 240.

19. Gilbert, p. 138.

20. Beth Bailey and David Farber, *The First Strange Place: The Alchemy of Race and Sex in World War II Hawaii* (New York: Free Press, 1992), pp. 105–106.

21. Clinton Sanders, *Customizing the Body: The Art and Culture of Tattooing* (Philadelphia: Temple University Press, 1989), pp. 18–19.

22. Tom Breitweg, interview with author Christine Whittington (November 1997).

23. Samuel M. Steward, *Bad Boys and Tough Tattoos: A Social History of the Tattoo with Gangs, Sailors, and Street-Corner Punks, 1950-1965* (New York: Harrington Park Press, 1990), p. 23.

24. MassInk.com, "The History" (http://www.massink.com/history.html)

25. Mariner's Museum, Newport News, *Skin Deep: The Art of Tattoo* (http://www.mariner.org/exhibits/tattoo/exhibit05.htm).

26. Arnold Rubin, "The Tattoo Renaissance," *Marks of Civilization: Artistic Transformations of the Human Body* (Los Angeles: Museum of Cultural History, University of California, 1989), p. 238.

27. Ellis Amburn, *Pearl: the Obsessions and Passions of Janis Joplin: A Biography* (New York: Warner Books, 1992), blurb on cover.

28. Rubin, pp. 233–252; Sanders, p. 1988.

29. Margo Mifflin, *Bodies of Subversion: A Secret History of Women and Tattoo* (San Francisco, Re/Search, 1997), p. 66.

30. Mifflin, pp. 148–150.

31. Mifflin, p. 150.

32. Lt. Jack Spratt, USN, interview with author Christine Whittington (April 2000).

33. Horace Beck, *Folklore and the Sea* (Mystic, CT: Mystic Seaport Museum, 1996, reprint ed., orig. 1973), p. 363.

34. Clinton R. Sanders, *Customizing the Body: The Art and Culture of Tattooing* (Philadelphia: Temple University Press, 1989), p. vii.

35. Karla Haworth, "Body Art Challenges Campus Health Centers," *Chronicle of Higher Education*, 19 (March 1999), p. A43.

Chapter 4

1. Victoria Lautman and Vicky Berndt (photographer). *The New Tattoo* (New York: Abbeville Press, 1994), p. 21.

2. Captain Bret's Tattoo Shop Inc., "Tribal Tattoo History & Symbolism," (http://www.tribal-celtic-tattoo.com/tribal-history.htm).

3. Lautman, p. 21–22.

4. V. Vale and A. Juno, *Modern Primitives: An Investigation of Contemporary Adornment and Ritual* (San Francisco: Re/Search Publications, 1989), p. 99.

5. Margo DeMello, *Bodies of Inscription: A Cultural History of the Modern Tattoo Community* (Durham, NC: Duke University Press, 2000), p. 65.

6. DeMello.

7. John Kinlein, interview with author Christine Whittington (April 2000).

8. Arnold Rubin, "The Tattoo Renaissance," *Marks of Civilization: Artistic Transformations of the Human Body* (Los Angeles: Museum of Cultural History, University of California, 1989), p. 233.

9. Lautman, p. 79.

10. Amy Krakow, *The Total Tattoo Book* (New York: Warner Books, 1994), p. 222.

11. Richard Stratton, introduction to Douglas Kent Hall, *Prison Tattoos* (New York: St. Martin's Press, 1997), p. 8.

12. Stratton in Hall, p. 7.

13. Hall, p. 8.

14. Hall.

15. Hall, pp. 12–13.

16. Mark S. Dunston, *Street Signs: An Identification Guide to Symbols of Crime and Violence* (Powers Lake, WI: Performance Dimensions, 1992), p. 112.

17. Hall, p. 10.

18. Hall, p. 11; Dunston, p. 64.

19. Dunston, p. 56.

20. Stratton in Hall, p. 7.

21. Steve Gilbert, *Tattoo History: A Source Book* (San Francisco: Juno Books, 2000), p. 9.

22. Gilbert, 103.

23. "Japanese Tattoo: History" (http://astro.temple.edu/~fdarling/history3.htm).

24. Kazuo Oguri, "Utagawa Kuniyoshi and the History of Japanese Tattoo Designs" (http://tattoos.com/oguri.htm).

25. *Tebori: Tattooing By Hand*, Abstract Arts (1999, http://abstractarts.com/tebori.htm).
26. Krakow, p. 53.
27. *AFU and Urban Legend Archives: Classic/Blue Star* Tattoos FAQ (The AFU and Urban Legends Archive, http://www.urbanlegends.com/classic/blue.star.tattoos/blue_star_lsd_faq.html).

Chapter 5

1. University of Pennsylvania Museum of Archaeology and Anthropology, "Piercing," *Body Modification Ancient and Modern* (http://www.upenn.edu/museum/Exhibits/bodmod-pierce.html).
2. University of Pennsylvania Museum of Archaeology.
3. V. Vale and A. Juno, *Modern Primitives: An Investigation of Contemporary Adornment and Ritual* (San Francisco: Re/Search Publications, 1989), p. 13.
4. Vale and Juno, p. 7.
5. Britannica.com, s.v. faquir, (http://www.britannica.com/eb/article?eu=34207&tocid=0).
6. *Encyclopedia Americana*, 1999 ed., s.v. "Fakir."
7. Daniel Mannix, *Memoirs of a Sword-Swallower* (San Francisco: Re/Search, 1996), p. 82.
8. Kim Hewitt, *Mutilating the Body: Identity in Blood and Ink* (Bowling Green, OH: Bowling Green State University Popular Press, 1997), pp. 109–110.
9. Jean-Chris Miller, *The Body Art Book: A Complete, Illustrated Guide to Tattoos, Piercings, and Other Body Modifications* (New York: Berkley Books, 1997), p. 92.
10. Hewitt, pp. 80; 87.
11. James Conroy, "James' Adventures in Piercing," *Daily Collegian*, Pennsylvania State University (http://www.collegian.psu.edu/archive/news_specials/piercing/piercing2.asp)

Chapter 6

1. "Bodies of Cultures: Tattooing," University of Pennsylvania Museum of Archaeology and Anthropology, (http://www.upenn.edu/museum/Exhibits/bodmodintro.html).
2. Australian Museum, "Aboriginal Scarification" (2000, http://www.austmus.gov.au/bodyart/scarring/indigenous.htm).
3. Yidumduma Bill Harnie, Wardaman Aboriginal Corporation, Northern Territory, Australian Museum's Body Art exhibit (http://www.austmus.gov.au/bodyart/scarring/indigenous.htm#top).
4. Robert Brain, *The Decorated Body* (Boston: Harper and Row, 1979), p. 70. Adranne Baker, "World Civilizations: A Workshop for Teachers" (June 24, 1998, http://www.csuohio.edu/history/courses/his380/baker/ body01.html).

5. Ben Lewis, "Body Art—Papua New Guinea Scarification," Australian Museum (2000 http://www.austmus.gov.au/bodyart/scarring/papua.htm).

6. University of Wisconsin—Green Bay, "Yoruba of Nigeria," (Anthropology 320 fall 1996 term project, http://www.uwgb.edu/galta/mrr/yoruba/home.htm#History_and_Origins). Also see Wayne RESA's Cultural Collaborative for Learning, "Scarification Teacher Guides Set #1: African Art Showing Adornment with Explanations" (http://resa.net/smart/dia/lesson7a.htm).

7. Margaret Grant (Webber Middle School, Detroit Public Schools), Wayne County (Michigan) Regional Educational Service Agency's Cultural Collaborative for Learning, "Social Studies Lesson: Scarification" (http://resa.net/smart/dia/lesson7.htm).

8. Grant.

9. Betty J. Meggers, *Amazonia: Man and Culture in a Counterfeit Paradise* (Chicago: Aldine Atherton, Inc., 1971), p. 77.

10. Texas Tech Health Sciences Center, Office of News and Publications, "Increasingly Popular Body Art Sometimes Borders on Self-Mutilation" (News release, March 9, 2000 http://www.ttuhsc.edu/pages/news&pub/release1-march00.html).

11. Lonnae O'Neal Parker, "Brand Identities," *Washington Post* (May 12, 1998, http://washingtonpost.com/wp-srv/style/features/brand.htm).

12. "Increasingly Popular Body Art Sometimes Borders on Self-Mutilation" (News release, March 9, 2000, http://www.ttuhsc.edu/pages/news&pub/release1-march00.html).

13. Body Modification Ezine site (http://bme.freeq.com/scar/bme-scar.html).

Chapter 7

1. American Dental Association, "ADA Statement on Intraoral/Perioral Piercing" (October 2000, http://www.ada.org/prof/prac/issues/statements/piercing.html)

2. KidsHealth, The Nemours Foundation, "Is Body Piercing Safe?" (http://kidshealth.org/teen/body_basics/body_piercing_safe.html).

3. Alliance of Professional Tattooists, "About APT" (http://www.safetattoos.com/about.htm).

4. Centers for Disease Control and Prevention, National Center for HIV, STD and TV Prevention, "Fact Sheet: HIV and Its Transmission" (January 31, 2001, http://www.cdc.gov/hiv/pubs/facts/transmission.htm).

5. Mayo Clinic Rochester (MN) online, "Common Disorders Seen by the Hepatobiliary Interest Group" (September 18, 2000, http://www.mayo.edu/int-med/gi/hepatobiliary.htm).

6. Eric Nagrouney, "Needle Can Add More Than Just a Tattoo," *The New York Times* (April 17, 2000, http://www.nyt.com).

7. Mayo Clinic Rochester News, "New Study Shows People with Heart Conditions Should Know Risks Associated with Body Piercing" (June 3, 1999, http://www.mayo.edu/comm/mcr/news/news_658.html).

8. "The Piercing Reality of Body Art," *NEA Today* (January 2001, http://www.nea.org/neatoday/0101/health.html).

9. Mike Balestrieri, "Tattoo Aftercare."

10. Mike Balestrieri, interview with author Kathlyn Gay (April 2001).

11. Margaret H. Christensen, Kathleen H. Miller, Carol A. Patsdaughter, and Lisa J. Dowd, "To the Point—The Contemporary Body Piercing and Tattooing Renaissance," Nursing Spectrum—Career Fitness Online (http://nsweb.nursingspectrum.com/ce/ce194.htm).

12. Anonymous interview with author Kathlyn Gay (May 2001).

13. "Force of Habit: Sister June Wilkerson's Tattoo Removal Project Helps Turn Troubled Lives Around," *People Weekly* (December 4, 2000), p. 99.

14. Salt Lake City Corporation, "Tattoo Removal Program," (http://www.ci.slc.ut.us/police/tattoos.htm).

Chapter 8

1. Gregory Weaver, Knight-Ridder Tribune Business News, "Employers Vary in Policies Toward Body Art, Piercings," *Indianapolis Star* (February 28, 2000).

2. Vince Cancasci, correspondence with author Kathlyn Gay (May 2001).

3. Anonymous interview with author Kathlyn Gay (May 2001).

4. Nancy Calaway, "Tattooed Officer Sues FW Chief in Heated Dispute," *Dallas Morning News* (July 23, 2001, http://txcn.com/dallasnews/425502_tattoocop_23me.html).

5. Joel Lurie Grishaver, "Randy's Navel Piercing," Teacher's Guide and Lesson Plan on Body Art (Los Angeles: Torah Aura Productions, 1999), p.2.

6. Grishaver.

7. Rabbi Barry H. Block, "Body Piercing, Tattoos, and the Image of God," sermon (April 24, 1998, http://www.beth-elsa.org/be_s0424.htm).

8. "Administrative Guidance to Army Tattoo Policy In Accordance With AR 670-1" (http://www.hood.army.mil/1cd_1-227cav/policy2.htm).

9. "Administrative Guidance to Army Tattoo Policy."

10. Rudi Williams, American Forces Press Service, "Walter Reed Lasers Blast Tattoos, Treat Other Conditions" (December 19, 2000, http://www.defenselink.mil/news/Dec2000/n12192000_200012192.html).

11. "Administrative Guidance to Army Tattoo Policy."

12. *Wear and Appearance of Army Uniforms and Insignia*, "Wearing of Jewelry, 1.14" (April 8, 1997, http://books.usapa.belvoir.army.mil/cgi-bin/bookmgr/BOOKS/R670_1/1.14).

13. Major James McGarrahan, correspondence with author Kathlyn Gay (April 2001).

14. "Naval Academy Skin Standards" (April 2, 2001, http://www.nadn.navy.mil/Admissions/medskin.htm).

15. USAF Academy Catalog 2000–2001, p. 157 (http://www.usafa.af.mil/rr/2000catalog/pg157.htm).

16. Law offices of George A. Boyle, "Tattoo and Body Piercing Laws," California Penal Code Section 652 (http://www.georgeboyle.com/tattoo.html).

17. Sara Rimensnyder, "Body Art (Massachusetts Law Against Tattooing is Overturned)," *Reason* (February 2001), p. 8.

18. Aaron Nicodemus, "Health Officials Firm Up Tattoo Regulations," *Standard-Times, SouthCoast Today* online (February 7, 2001, http://www.s-t.com/daily/02-01/02-07-01/a07lo043.htm).

Chapter 9

1. John Wilton, "Toward an Understanding of Skin Art," D. Blandy and K. Congdon, *Pluralistic Approaches to Art Criticism* (Bowling Green, OH: Bowling Green State University Popular Press, 1991, http://www.accad.ohio-ate.edu/~dkrug/367/online/ethnicarts4/r_resources/reading/Wilton.asp).

Index